Our World was in
BLACK & WHITE

More Colorful Essays of
"Growing Up North"

by Jerry Harju

Our World was in
BLACK & WHITE

More Colorful Essays of
"Growing Up North"

by Jerry Harju

Cover Design by Stacey Willey
Edited by Karen Murr and Pat Green

Copyright 2006
Jerry Harju

Published by North Harbor Publishing
Marquette, Michigan

Publishing Coordination by
Globe Printing, Inc.
Ishpeming, Michigan

Printed by Sheridan Books, Ann Arbor, Michigan

ISBN 0-9670205-9-X
Library of Congress Control Number 2005937793

March 2006

INTRODUCTION

This book is a collection of my columns published in the *Mining Journal*, Upper Michigan's largest newspaper. These essays aren't indictments of national politics or the world condition, although I do take a few potshots at our intrepid government. I mostly write about what I remember as a kid—fun stuff, really.

The group on the cover is the Hole-in-the-Woodpile Gang from South Ishpeming, circa 1942. That's me in the center with the blonde pumpkin-size Charley Brown head. As you can see, we never went anywhere unless we were heavily armed. I don't remember why Mary Ann Ombrello had a broom instead of a pistol. Maybe she wanted it that way. In any event the broom was much more lethal than our guns.

Jerry Harju
North Harbor Publishing
528 E. Arch St.
Marquette, MI 49855
Toll Free (877) 906-3984
E-mail: jharju@chartermi.net
Website: www.jerryharju.com

DEDICATION

To all my readers, bless their excellent taste.

ACKNOWLEDGMENTS

I, alone, could not have produced this book; a lot of help was necessary. Karen Murr and Pat Green, my word-police editors, repaired the horrible punctuation and punched up the prose so it became halfway readable. While lunching at Peggy Sue's Café, my good friend, Jeff Jacobs, has repeatedly jogged my memory about our kidhood misdeeds. I have to thank my ex-wife, Joanne, for playing a key role in the bizarre twists of a few of these essays. Many thanks to Stacey Willey, the Adobe Photoshop wizard at Globe Printing, for suffering through one hundred and ninety-seven modifications of the book's cover design. As usual, Steve Schmeck was kind enough to do the book's bar codes. Kathy McMonagle and Jean Schroeder at downstate Sheridan Books pitched in and got the book printed and on the street. Finally, special appreciation to the staff at the *Mining Journal* in Marquette, Michigan, for initially publishing all of this material.

CONTENTS

Books by Jerry Harju

SNOWSUIT MEMORIES

One gratifying thing about not being young anymore is that I can wear clothes that actually fit.

As a kid I didn't have any say about what I wore or what size it was. My mother made sure that every stitch of clothing she bought for me was six sizes too large. "You'll grow into it," she said, as I stood there in huge new BVD's while she cinched up the waistband with a safety pin. Not only did I grow into clothes, I was also forced to grow out of them. Everything I wore had to last at least three years. There was only one day during that three-year period when my shirt actually fit just right.

In order to hold up a very large pair of pants I had to wear suspenders. Other kids considered you a pathetic, snot-nose little dweeb if you wore suspenders to keep your pants from falling down. But what was really the worst, the ultimate excommunication from civilized kid society, was having to wear suspenders to hold up corduroy knickers. You were instantly classified as a lower order pea-brain specie that went "skritch, skritch, skritch" as it moved. It was a supreme effort to walk so that the knickers legs wouldn't rub together. I was convinced that bowlegged cowboys in the Saturday-afternoon matinees must have learned to walk that way because their mothers made them wear corduroy knickers when they were kids.

The one thing I really wanted to wear I never got. Around 1940 men's knee-high leather boots were very popular. They were called high tops. I found a dandy pair in the Montgomery Ward catalog with twenty shiny metal lace hooks on each boot. Best of all, one boot had a nifty leather pocket on the calf to hold your jackknife! I had to have those boots because they looked so neat, and it's in the genes of Finn males to carry a knife in their boot. But my mother was having none of it. "Those boots cost over five dollars," she said. "I can buy you a brand new suit for less than that!" I told her that I'd wear corduroy knickers for the rest of my life if I could just have a pair of those boots. But she stood firm, and I never got them.

There were a lot of clothes I wore in the winter that I hated with a passion. Who could forget the notorious snowsuit? The snowsuit was a hooded one-piece affair with a zipper up the front, made from wool thick enough to deflect bullets. But that wasn't enough for my mother. Underneath the snowsuit she made me wear long underwear, knickers of course, a woolen shirt, two pairs of heavy socks, and at least two sweaters. Attached to each other through the snowsuit sleeves were the infamous "mittens on a string." Completing the ensemble were five-pound rubber galoshes and a fifteen-foot woolen scarf tightly wound around my head and face. All this took an hour to put on, and once you were suited up God help you if you had to go to the toilet. You were doomed. Once outside another danger lurked. If you fell down while encased in your snowsuit, there was no way in the world you were going to get back up without help. You would just lie there in the snow, helplessly waving your arms and legs like an overturned turtle. There are Yoopers who still wake up in the middle of the night in a cold sweat, remembering when they fell over in their snowsuits.

There was one thing I had to wear as a kid which, to this day, I've never admitted to anyone. I wore a garter belt. That's right, a garter belt. Since the knickers only came down to my knees, I wore thigh-high brown woolen stockings with them. The stockings didn't have elastic tops so my mother claimed that a garter belt was necessary to keep them up. Actually, it was really a garter harness with straps around the shoulders and waist. All very humiliating for a young, strapping U.P. lad.

Ahh . . . I feel much better now that I've got that off my chest. If any of you guys had the same experience with garters when you were a kid, let me know. You'll feel better. We could even form an anonymous club and talk it out.

ℰᏕ

REMEMBERING "THE FUNNIES"

I realized something interesting while reading the comics in the Sunday *Mining Journal* recently. Blondie is the only comic strip that's survived throughout my lifetime. Blondie first appeared in 1930, three years before I was born, and the strip is still going strong. There are some interesting but not-well-known facts about the early Blondie strip. When it first began, Dagwood and Blondie weren't married. Blondie's maiden name was—are you ready for this?—Boopadoop. She was a flighty flapper who began dating playboy (that's what I said, playboy) Dagwood Bumstead, heir to the Bumstead Locomotive Works fortune. Dagwood fell madly in love with the pretty Miss Boopadoop and told his father that he was going to marry her. The elder Bumstead objected strongly, claiming that Blondie was beneath their social position. When the love-struck couple got married in 1933, Dagwood was disinherited by his irate father and had to join the working class. Who says that love doesn't conquer all?

I'm glad to see that in recent years Dagwood finally got rid of that white shirt with the huge button in the center. I could never figure out what that dumb button was all about.

Speaking of early comics, or funnies as we called them, Blondie and Dagwood lived a life of total wedded bliss compared to husbands and wives in other strips. In Bringing Up Father, Jiggs, an Irish-American bricklayer, and his laundress wife, Maggie, found themselves suddenly very wealthy, courtesy of a lucky lottery ticket. Maggie immediately attempted to scramble up the social ladder, buying expensive clothes and cars and throwing lavish parties in their newly acquired mansion. Jiggs was having none of it. He clung to a fondness for cheap cigars, corned beef and cabbage, and lapping up beer with his old cronies. Maggie tried to make him see the error of his ways but to no avail. Her thin veneer of respectability often shattered, resulting in a blizzard of rolling pins, crockery, and expensive vases ricocheting off Jiggs' skull.

Another comic-strip marriage not made in heaven was Major and Martha Hoople in Our Boarding House. Martha, built like a Sherman tank with a disposition to match, ran the boarding house while Major Hoople, an overweight, cigar-smoking, work-avoiding windbag, bent the boarders' ears with long discourses of his fictional heroics in the Boer War. Martha's patience with the Major's laziness often ran thin, and she'd grab her weapon of choice—a frying pan—and smack him across the head.

Physical aggression between family members was commonplace in early comic strips. In The Katzenjammer Kids, a German family, Mama Katzenjammer and her small twin sons, Hans and Fritz, were, for some mysterious reason, living on a tropical island with a live-in companion, Der Captain. Der Captain, although not married to Mama Katzenjammer, readily assumed the father role and regularly and enthusiastically whaled the tar out of the boys for real and imagined disobediences. But Hans and Fritz, the urchins from hell, were resilient, and they set up highly elaborate and dangerous pranks to exact revenge and possibly even shorten Der Captain's life. They never succeeded, of course, and the strip ran for decades.

One of my personal favorites was Smokey Stover, who was—what else?—a fireman. The strip plots were pretty lame, but it was filled with puns and other subtle word play that were fun to figure out, e.g., the license plate on the fire truck was FOOE2U.

And since I've always been in love with rockets and space, another strip I really liked was Buck Rogers. When I was small and my reading skills weren't well developed I'd ask my father to read the funnies to me. The old man would do that, but he never liked Buck Rogers, claiming that there wasn't anything funny about it, and that "all that future stuff" was unbelievable. Interestingly though, much of "that future stuff" that appeared in Buck Rogers are now scientific facts—atomic energy, television, lasers, rocket bombs, and hovercraft.

But my all-time absolute favorite comic strip was Li'l Abner. Cartoonist Al Capp created an immensely rich cast of characters and unforgettable situations. Who could forget Li'l Abner's mom, the corncob-pipe-smoking Mammy Yokum, strong enough to flatten Popeye no matter how much spinach he wolfed down. With her lethal right uppercut—the "good-night-Irene punch,"—Mammy upheld law and order in hometown Dogpatch, maintaining that "good is better'n evil 'cause it's nicer."

Capp created a comic strip within a comic strip. Li'l Abner's "ideel" was Fearless Fosdick, a comic strip he faithfully read every day. A lantern-jawed detective, Fearless Fosdick appeared to be Dick Tracy's dumber brother. While Tracy occasionally suffered a gunshot wound at the hands of some arch-criminal, Fearless Fosdick's trademark was a Swiss-cheese body from all the bullets he took. Although he had the IQ of a turnip and was horribly underpaid, Fosdick unflinchingly upheld the law and somehow managed to nab the bad guys.

Capp also introduced a holiday still observed in many U.S. locales to this day. Sadie Hawkins Day, named after "the homeliest gal in the Dogpatch hills," featured a foot race that allowed the Dogpatch old maids to pursue all of the town's bachelors with matrimony as the prize. Some of the underhanded tactics that these women employed to slow down the petrified males still makes my blood run cold.

I was discussing old comic-strip characters with my friend Jeff, and he stated that there was one mystery that bothers him to this day. Clark Kent always entered a telephone booth to remove his outer clothes to become Superman. But Superman never returned to the booth to pick up Clark's stuff. What happened to those clothes? Did homeless people grab them? Did they wind up at the Salvation Army? And did the Daily Planet buy Clark Kent a new suit every day? I think not. If anyone can shed some light on this issue, email me at jharju@chartermi.net.

ॐ

WHAT'S IN A NICKNAME?

I can't speak for younger generations, but when I was a kid in the U.P. every man and boy had a nickname. They were so commonly used that you often didn't know a guy's real name. I remember sitting in the Republic High School assembly room, and the school superintendent, Guy Schutte, at the front of the room, would point his long, bony finger at a student and bark out, "Walter, quit daydreaming and tend to your assignments!"

We'd all look up and gaze around, wondering who the heck Walter was. Only later we'd find out that Walter was the kid we all knew as Piggy.

If you were a U.P. baby boy baptized with a respectable, multi-syllable name like Jonathan, Edward, Clarence, or Reginald, the chances of that name surviving puberty were nil. By then you'd be Punk, Chebbu, Buckshot, or Pickle.

When I was in high school my nickname was Cruncher. In the tenth-grade English class we were reading "The Tale of Two Cities," which had a character named Jerry Cruncher. From then on I was Cruncher. Oh, incidentally, the Cruncher in the Dickens' novel was a resurrectionist, that is, a grave robber.

My friend, Jeff Jacobs, has several nicknames. When we were little, he was known as Kippy. Some people now call him Jake or

JJ. He says he has other names, but they can't be mentioned in polite company.

That's true of many U.P. nicknames. Some of them are so "colorful" that they can't be printed in a family newspaper, so I'll only discuss the ones that are still colorful but rated PG.

Nicknames often reflect personal quirks. There was a guy in Republic who hung around with his pals at the local gas station. Whenever somebody was eating a candy bar he'd ask, "Hey, kin I have a hunk'a that?" They began calling him Hunka.

Another fellow had a habit of clicking his false teeth. His friends labeled him "Jaws."

Tom Sullivan was a legendary character who roamed around the Big Bay area in the early 1900's. Sullivan referred to anything or anybody that he considered second rate as "tin can." He quit work at the Lake Independence Lumber Company because it was "a tin can outfit." Soon he became known as Tin Can Sullivan, a name that stuck with him for the rest of his life.

Nicknames also described what you did. Years ago Earl Arola ran a soft-drink plant in Republic. They called him Pop Jack. One fellow trapped beaver and mink for a living, so naturally he was called Trapper. His son also wound up being called Trapper even though he didn't trap a thing. Another guy, a mechanic, had a last name of Tuomi. One of his pals was inspired to dub him Socket. (Socket Tuomi, get it?).

If you were unlucky, you'd be tagged with a nickname that may or may not have described how you looked, and I don't mean Handsome. You might have been called Tiny, Porky, Pimples, Big Butt, Grubby, or even Bottlenose.

Many of the nicknames you hear in the U.P. are Finnish. Guys, especially Finns, might get tagged with monikers like Makkara (sausage), Rapa (dirt), or Liha (meat).

Over time I've received lists of nicknames from people I know.

Many thanks to Barb Laurila, Leo and Elaine Nirva, Paul and Monica Tessmer, and Marilyn Helmila. For you nickname buffs, here are some of the better ones. I know many of the people to whom these nicknames are attached, but I'm keeping my mouth shut about the identities.

Choker, Kissy, Stiggy, Sunshine, Smudge, Monkey, Peanut, Peewee, Sluggo, Squeaky, Bullet Shoes, Peachy, Moose, Haybelly, Otter, Hooch, Catsy, Mousey, Sliver, Donut, Beetle, Redball, Stretch, Stubby, Camshaft, Lumpy, Punk, Jellybean, Hummer, Skuffer, Jughead, Beak, Crabber, Plutz, Soupy, Numbers, Bootsy, Pippy, Chippy, Sarge, Bandsaw, Pork Chop, Bucko, Budda, Pud, Wimpy, Burlap, Applesauce, Nine Toes, Nuz, Itchy, Corny, Pusky, Crabber, Snoose, Buttercup, Poodle, Chinky, Beaver, Poopoo, Pogey, Snooky, Weiner, Inky, Ticky, Titter, Bowser, Crud, Scoofer, Berf, Blob, Nubby, and Moona.

So, there you are. If you have or know of a nickname that has a lot of class (by that I really mean lack of class), email them to me at jharju@chartermi.net. This is Jerry (a.k.a. Cruncher) Harju signing off.

୫୦ଓଓ

THE U.P. — TRULY SOMEPLACE SPECIAL

Angie Cristan of TV6 called me up, asking if I would do an interview in support of the 25th anniversary of Upper Michigan's "Someplace Special" slogan. I didn't know what was involved, but I agreed to do it.

I met Angie and a TV6 cameraman at Presque Isle to shoot the interview. When the camera got rolling, the first question I was asked was, "What are the things you like about the U.P.?"

I fumbled around, trying to answer the question. Now, after giving it some thought, I've come up with a more comprehensive list of reasons why the U.P. is truly "Someplace Special" for me.

After being brought up in the U.P., I spent much of my life in the Los Angeles area in California. I've only been back here since 1996. In order to really appreciate the quality of life in the U.P. I believe that you have to live somewhere else for a period of time.

For example, Yoopers take our clean air pretty much for granted. Clean air is in short supply in big cities. Los Angelinos are so accustomed to smog that they would get very nervous in the U.P. because they don't trust air they can't see. It's getting so bad out there that when the swallows of Capistrano return to California in the spring they now carry tiny inhalers around their necks.

There aren't many people living in Upper Michigan, which is just fine with me. No traffic jams. In Los Angeles people spend so much of their lives sitting in traffic jams that they have to make use of that time or they'll never get anything done. Commuters sit behind the wheel conducting business on cell phones, eating breakfast, shaving, doing their nails, reading the Los Angeles Times, or taking graduate courses on their laptop computers.

Yoopers don't have to wait in line for anything. In the big cities there are long lines everywhere. You wait in line to get seated in a restaurant, buy a ticket to a movie, cash a check at the bank, buy gas, or even to pick up dry cleaning. When I lived in Marina del Rey—and I'm not making this up—people would begin gathering in a line at the post office door a half hour before it opened so they wouldn't have to wait in line at the window.

There's very little crime in the U.P. I like going for my walk before the sun comes up and not having to worry about being mugged. I can drive over to Shopko, park my Subaru, and go into the store leaving the car unlocked with the engine running. Do that in California and by the time you come out of the store the car will be halfway to Mexico where it will be disassembled and sold for parts.

I like the four seasons up here. There's nothing better than driving along the back roads in early October and taking in the fall colors. In the winter I enjoy walking around east Marquette when snow is falling. I have to admit that Southern California has four seasons, too—fire, flood, riots, and earthquakes.

Speaking of earthquakes, in January, 1994, when I was living in Marina del Rey, I was up early one morning, getting dressed for my morning jog, when the now-famous Northridge earthquake hit—a nasty 6.7 rumbler. All my books flew off the shelves, the TV leaped up and fell on the floor, and then the power went out. I fumbled around and found a flashlight and went out and knocked on the door of the apartment across the hall. A guy timidly opened the door a crack, but kept the chain on, thinking that I was a looter getting an early start. I had lived there for three years, but we'd never met. I introduced myself and told him that I wanted to find out if he was all right. He said that he was okay and then closed the door. We never saw each other again. That's the way it is with neighbors in the big city.

It's not like that up here. Not only do you know your neighbors, but you typically become friends with them. In fact—and this almost never happens in the big city—I've also become friends with many people I do business with. One day I drove over to Heritage Motors to get my car washed, but the fellow who usually washes cars was at lunch. Dick Lutey, the co-owner of Heritage, came out of his office, drove my car to the back and hand washed it himself. A month after I bought my new Subaru I went out one morning to find the battery dead. I called Crown Motors and spoke to Deb Danielson, the salesperson who sold it to me. She came right over with a battery pack, jump started my car, and pointed out that the map light had been accidentally left on. A week ago one of my neighbors in my apartment house couldn't get a new printer hooked up to her computer. I called up Mike Hainstock who repairs computers at Radio Shack in Ishpeming. The next morning, on his way to work, Mike stopped over and installed the printer.

These folks didn't have to do what they did, it's not in their job description. But that's the way people are up here, and I love it.

These are some of the many reasons that I live in the U.P. I'm restricted for space here, or I could come up with more. If you still think you'd prefer someplace like sunny Los Angeles because we get too much snow up here, then I suggest you hop on a plane and fly out there to check it out. Stay a few weeks to get the real flavor. Better buy a round-trip ticket, though.

∽∾

HELMI'S SECRET

I came across a Victoria's Secret catalog the other day. After leafing through it for an hour or two (not a regular habit of mine, of course) it's my opinion that no clear-thinking Upper Michigan woman would be interested in buying such impractical apparel. The so-called clothing Victoria's Secret sells, while projecting a certain amount of sex appeal, offers absolutely no protection against the elements. A mesh babydoll weighing in at a tenth of a gram may go over big in Miami Beach, Beverly Hills, or Honolulu where wind chill factors are eighty-five degrees above zero, but how about Upper Michigan in January? When the furnace struggles to raise the bedroom temperature out of the fifties, no woman in her right mind would opt to wear some filmy nothing to bed no matter how much she wants to arouse her husband. Goosebumps are not erotic.

But will Victoria's Secret alter their fashion line for northern climates? I think not. They have absolutely no idea what life is like during a northern winter. This presents a marvelous opportunity for someone up here to introduce a line of women's intimate apparel that's sensible, yet alluring.

Picture this.

The scene is the Berry Event Center in Marquette. The house lights are down, but baby spotlights travel up and down a long runway projecting from a curtained stage. A blizzard is raging outside, but the center is packed with an eager audience of women. Edgy, fast-paced music is playing in the background.

A female voice comes over the audio system. "Ladies, welcome to Helmi's Secret! Winter fashions for the U.P. woman!"

Suddenly the runway is ablaze with light. The curtains part. A comely but deadpan young lady steps out on stiletto heels, hand on hip, placing one foot in front of the other as she boldly strides down the runway.

The voice on the audio system describes the action. "Brigette is our first model. Bo Peep hasn't lost her sheep. She's got them right inside Helmi's Secret state-of-the-art Bo Peep bra. The Bo Peep bra features a thick sheepskin lining, affording maximum warmth while providing every woman with full-figure luxury. Frostbitten fingers can easily manipulate the front-closure clasp. You will notice that Brigette also wears the color-coordinated sheepskin-lined panties and earmuffs and sexy polypropylene-insulated thigh-length stockings."

The audience applauds in appreciation.

Another model takes the runway.

"Yvonne is wearing Helmi's Electric Teddy. This innovative and provocative piece has a portable nickel-cadmium power pack that activates heating elements throughout the garment to help keep those romantic moments nice and cozy. It also features lacy front pockets for optional electric hand heaters. Woolen leg warmers in stripes or plaids complete the ensemble."

A third model walks onto the runway. A low, drawn-out gasp issues from the audience. Several women scream with shock.

"No, ladies, Cherise is not nude. She is modelling Helmi's latest creation, the Long Jane, a scientific breakthrough in undergarments. As you can see, the Long Jane is one piece, extending from neck to ankle, with full-length sleeves, made from a NASA-designed soft, smooth spandex material with the consistency and appearance of real flesh. It is available in a variety of skin tones. In subdued light and after a glass of wine or two, your romantic partner will not know if he is touching the real you or the Long Jane. No longer will you have to shiver through those long winter evenings in a chilly bedroom. The Long Jane will provide the ultimate in comfort."

A puzzled woman in the audience puts up her hand. "But . . .but . . . if it's all one piece . . . how? . . ."

The announcer chuckles. "Rest assured, ladies, following a decades-old French design, concealed flaps make the Long Jane convenient and anatomically correct."

So, there you have it. Okay, so maybe I'm NOT an authority on the subject, but you have to admit that some enterprising U.P. woman could certainly show Victoria's Secret how to blaze new frontiers in women's fashions.

ഇൻൽ

YOOPER FEAR FACTOR

I hate to reveal this sordid fact of my personal life, but from time to time I have watched Fear Factor, the NBC reality show. Fear Factor doesn't give Masterpiece Theater any serious competition for intellectual stimulation, but I tune in anyway, mainly because the female contestants are carefully selected for the way they can fill out a tank top.

Substantial prize money drives people to compete against one another in stunts that would scare the (s-word) out of ordinary citizens. For example, a hunky guy is dropped from a fifty-foot-high helicopter into deep water to rescue his girlfriend who is handcuffed and going under the waves for the third time. Or she might be placed in a glass coffin and covered with live tarantulas. The coffin is then closed and locked, and her guy has to retrieve the key by sucking it through a large tube filled with a tasty beverage made from vinegar and mashed crickets in order to get the coffin open before she goes completely psycho.

To keep the ratings up, Fear Factor stunts, over the weeks, have become more dangerous and demeaning. Last Monday a group of good-looking young ladies were racing against each other, filling up a pail with live nightcrawlers, cow's brains, and ground up pig uterus. They had to bring this assortment of goodies to the pail with—are you ready for this?—their mouths. Doesn't that make you want to run to the refrigerator for a snack?

Fear Factor challenges here in the U.P. would have plenty of excitement and risk but not be nearly as gross as a mouthful of pig uterus. After all, we Yoopers have our dignity.

Picture a camp on the frozen Michigamme River in mid-January. The air temperature is twenty below zero. A stiff, frigid wind blows off the river, making an eerie moaning sound as it rushes through the pine trees.

Several technicians are standing in the snow, pointing bright lights and a camera at nine people shivering outside the cabin. The program host is speaking into the camera.

"This is Yooper Fear Factor, coming to you from the heart of Michigan's Upper Peninsula. Folks, it's really cold up here. All of our eight contestants come from much warmer locales, and right now they're really suffering.

"Our participants will now change into swimwear and enter the sauna in this cabin. They will remain in the sauna—with a temperature of 200 degrees—for thirty minutes. Then the clock will begin. These people must rush outside and jump into a snowbank, then hurry back into the cabin where they'll attempt to pour brandy into a shot glass and drink it down. The six people with the quickest times will go on. Anyone falling to the snow in a state of thermal shock will be eliminated. You viewers may find it incredible, but this strange and perilous activity was part of the Finnish culture up here for many decades. They happily went through it every Saturday night."

The challenge begins. The first participant, a young man in Speedo trunks, rushes into the cabin from his plunge into the snowbank. Parts of his body are steaming, and other parts are covered with glittering frost. He has a vacant wild stare, and his trembling lips are rapidly turning blue. He makes a wild grab for the brandy bottle but can't hang on, and it falls to the floor. On the fourth attempt he manages to slop enough brandy into a shot glass, but his hands are shaking so badly that he can't find his mouth. He finally collapses to the floor in a quivering heap.

Another challenge. On the edge of a cedar swamp in early June, the Yooper Fear Factor participants, dressed in skimpy bikinis and abbreviated trunks, await instructions from the host. An ominous humming is heard from the swamp.

The host announces, "People, your challenge here is to proceed through this swamp along a mile-long path to the other side. You may swat the mosquitoes with your hands, but you will carry no insect repellant. Each of you will wear heavy ankle weights to prevent a large swarm of mosquitoes from carrying you off. Those who panic and leave the swamp without completing the course will be eliminated from further competition. Anyone who cannot leave the swamp under their own power due to weakness caused by loss of blood will also be eliminated. Okay folks, let's go!"

The contestants rush down the path into the swamp. Immediately the humming becomes louder. A piercing scream comes from the swamp.

And here's a fitting season-finale episode. Picture the woods on a chill mid-November morning. Numerous rifle shots and loud excited voices can be heard from the forest. Four final participants listen to the host's instructions.

"Okay, folks, this is the final Yooper Fear Factor challenge. Today one of you will take home one million dollars. So, here's the situation. Today is the first day of firearm deer season . . ."

A female participant interrupts. "Oh, no! I can't do this! I love animals! I won't shoot a deer!"

The host chuckles. "You misunderstand. You won't have a rifle. We're going to issue each of you a bulletproof vest and a Kevlar helmet. You see, the hunters in this immediate area are from Chicago, Detroit, and other urban areas. They come up here, not so much to hunt deer but to get away from their wives and drink with their buddies. These guys have been sucking up the sauce all night long, and now they're out here with loaded weapons. Each of you will have a compass, and the challenge is to be the first to arrive at our checkpoint one mile directly north of you without sustaining gunshot wounds that will halt your progress . . ."

The four finalists charge into the woods. Immediately more rifle fire breaks out. A hunter shouts excitedly. "Hey Ralph, there's a herd of four of them headed your way! I think I might'a winged one of 'em!"

഻ଓ

ALL ABOUT MOM

D o you remember what you thought about your mother when you were a kid? No? The following school-age children's answers to questions about moms may help refresh your memory.

Why did God make mothers?
1. It was the best way to get more people.
2. Mostly to clean the house.
3. To help us out of there when we were getting born.
4. She's the only one who knows where the Scotch tape is.

How did God make mothers?
1. He used dirt, just like for the rest of us.
2. Magic plus super powers and a lot of string.
3. God make my mom just the same like he made me. He just used bigger parts.

Why did God give you your mother and not some other mom?
1. Because we're related.
2. God knew she likes me a lot more than other people's moms like me.

What ingredients are mothers make of?
1. God makes mothers out of clouds and angel hair and everything nice in the world and one dab of mean.
2. They had to get their start from men's bones. Then they used mostly string, I think.

What kind of little girl was your mom?
1. My mom has always been my mom and none of that other stuff.
2. I don't know because I wasn't there, but my guess would be pretty bossy.
3. They say she used to be pretty nice.

How did your mom meet your dad?
1. Mom was working in a store and dad was shoplifting.

What did mom need to know about dad before she married him?
1. His last name.
2. She had to know his background. Like is he a crook? Does he get drunk on beer? Does he make at least $800 a year? Did he say no to drugs and yes to chores?

Why did your mom marry your dad?
1. My dad makes the best spaghetti in the world, and my mom eats a lot.
2. She got too old to do anything else with him.
3. My grandma says that mom didn't have her thinking cap on.

What makes a real mother?
1. It means you have to be really bossy without looking bossy.

Who's the boss at your house?
1. Mom doesn't want to be boss, but she has to because dad's such a goofball.
2. Mom. You can tell by room inspection. She sees stuff under the bed.
3. I guess Mom is, but only because she has a lot more to do than dad.

What's the difference between moms and dads?
1. Moms work at work and work at home, and dads just got to work at work.
2. Moms know how to talk to teachers without scaring them.
3. Dads are taller and stronger, but moms have all the real power because that's who you gotta ask if you want to sleep over at friends.

What does your mom do in her spare time?
1. Mothers don't do spare time.
2. To hear her tell it, she pays bills all day long.

What's the difference between moms and grandmas?
1. About 30 years.
2. You can always count on grandmothers for candy.

Describe the world's perfect mom.
1. She would make broccoli taste like ice cream.
2. The greatest mom in the world wouldn't make me kiss my fat aunts.
3. She'd always be smiling and keep her opinions to herself.

Is anything about your mom perfect?
1. Her teeth are perfect, but she bought them from the dentist.
2. Her casserole recipes, but we hate them.
3. Just her children.

What would it take to make your mom absolutely perfect?
1. On the inside she's already perfect. Outside, I think some kind of plastic surgery.
2. Diet. And her hair. I'd dye it, maybe blue.

If you could change one thing about your mom, what would it be?
1. She has this weird thing about me keeping my room clean. I'd get rid of that.
2. I'd make my mom smarter. Then she'd know it was my sister who did it and not me.

෨෬

WAGING A CASH-AND-CARRY WAR

I've been logging in a lot of time watching CNN where Bush and Kerry are involved in intellectually stimulating discussions on whether or not Kerry threw his Vietnam medals over the fence or was it just his ribbons and how many times Bush played hookey from his 1970's Air National Guard duty. Isn't it exhilarating to know that one of these gentlemen will be our fearless leader next year?

One particular subject that you won't find either one of them bringing up in this election year is the National Debt. I'm sure most of you know that the National Debt is what our nation owes various organizations and people (e.g., banks, insurance companies, private citizens) who've lent our government money over the years. Everyone is also aware that this debt is a somewhat large number. But how large is it? The National Debt is over seven trillion—a seven followed by twelve zeros—dollars. And it's climbing. In the short time it's taken me to scribble down these two paragraphs the debt has risen by seven million dollars. I'm not kidding. If you want to see this for yourself bring up U. S. National Debt Clock.com on the Internet.

Why does the National Debt keep increasing? The answer is simple enough. Our intrepid government keeps borrowing money faster than it pays off its loans. And don't blame it all on the Republican administration. During the past several decades the Democrats have demonstrated that they're equally up to the task of deficit spending.

Why do our legislators do this? Simple. A politician in office must spend tons of money on pork-barrel projects to keep his constituents happy so they'll vote for him at the next election. No politician in his so-called right mind would ever consider paying down the National Debt because it's a boring way to spend money, and bored voters tend to vote for someone else. It's probably dawning on you about now that if you monitored your personal spending the same way the U.S. government runs the federal budget you'd be living under a bridge in a cardboard box.

The nastiest thing about this humongous debt is the interest. For Fiscal Year 2004 the U.S. government will have to pay over 460 BILLION dollars in interest on the National Debt. This is real money I'm talking about. When you pay your Federal income tax next April 15, over $1500 of your hard-earned tax money will go toward the interest payment on the National Debt. If you have a spouse and two kids, then your family's share will be over $6000.

My father thought that borrowing money and paying interest on the loan was the stupidest thing he ever heard of. I was brought up in an environment where there was no such thing as debt. My parents bought the house I was born in for cash. I don't think that either my mother or father saw the inside of a bank while I was growing up. They never even had a checking account. Every transaction was cash and carry. If they wanted something but couldn't afford it, then they didn't buy it until they had the money. There was never a bill in our mailbox. I saved quarters, half dollars, and dollar bills for two years to buy my first car. If I had asked my old man to loan me the money to buy it, he would have laughed me right out of the house.

As you may have guessed by now, war is another major factor in driving up the National Debt. For the years 2003 and 2004, Congress has approved $170 billion dollars for operations in Iraq and Afghanistan, and no one knows what it will cost next year. That's the trouble with war, you never know what the final price tag will be.

Our government should borrow a page from my old man's book and conduct war on a cash and carry basis. Only wage war as long as we can pay for it. If the U.S. armed forces got strapped for cash and couldn't buy any more tanks, guns, or fighter planes, then the war would come to a grinding halt.

"Ladies and gentlemen, this just in from our CNN reporter at the Pentagon. A cease fire has just been declared in Iraq because U.S troops have run out of bullets. The President is issuing a special plea to all taxpayers to immediately send in a check for two thousand dollars to buy more ammunition . . . "

"Helmi, did'ja hear that? The President wants us to send him money to keep the war going."

"Is he kidding? Not a chance! We gotta buy a new snow blower this winter!"

§◯Ռ

FILL 'ER UP . . . OR MAYBE NOT

These days talking heads on TV are spouting sage advice on how to deal with the sky-high price of gasoline, like reducing our dependence on foreign oil or more research on condensation of gasoline from natural gas. But does that egghead advice help when you're filling up your SUV this summer? I don't think so. Short-term, practical measures are needed. When I was in high school in Republic and first began driving, we had a few down-to-earth ways to reduce driving expenses.

Most of the times I drove my Model A were when I was either taking out a girl or looking for a girl to take out. I never had extra gas for frivolous trips like going back and forth to school. If I had a Saturday-night date with some tenth-grade sweetie, I had to finance the whole operation on about fifty cents. Two hamburgers with fries cost thirty cents, two Cokes, ten cents, leaving a dime for gas. My date would have thought I was pretty cheap if I'd only put ten cents worth of gas in the car, so we usually double dated. The guy in the back seat would chip in a dime, and we'd splurge with twenty cents' worth of gas.

The most desirable girls were those who liked to have their hamburger and Coke and then go and park. This was generally a lot of fun and really saved on gas. I never took out gold diggers who wanted to drive down to Ishpeming for a movie. I couldn't afford the gasoline OR the movie.

One trick to conserve gas was to adjust the engine's idling speed down to one notch above stalling. If I slowed the car to chat up some cutie walking along a Republic street, I didn't want to burn up a lot of gas while trying to talk her into going for a ride.

Another way we saved gas was coasting down hills. Before Cleveland Cliff rearranged the topography of Republic there was a long hill south of town leading to Park City, a tiny Republic suburb. I was taking out a Park City girl for awhile, and I'd always kill the engine and coast down the hill when we were heading back into town. She never asked me why I did that. I think she thought it was romantic.

There were shifty ways of getting free gas. One was draining the gas-pump hoses at the filling stations. I don't think it works with these modern electronic pumps, but on the old pumps, when they weren't being used, there was always gasoline left in the loop in the hose. I used to drive up to the pumps, preferably after the station closed, put the nozzle in the Model A's gas tank, hold the hose high over my head and drain the residual hose gas into my tank. Kind of like checking the coin slot on a public telephone. With luck I could get a half pint from each hose. A half pint here, a half pint there, it all added up.

The other way to get free gas was more than just shifty, it was highly illegal. When we had no money but absolutely had to get some gasoline to get back home, we occasionally resorted to siphoning. As you might guess, siphoning gasoline was strictly a nocturnal activity. It required four things: a six-foot length of rubber hose, a gas can, a funnel, and a stranger's parked car, preferably on an unlighted street. With one end of the hose in the parked car's gas tank and the other end in your mouth, you sucked gasoline up into the hose to get the siphon started and then quickly put that end into the can to be filled. This was usually a two-man operation, one guy sucking gas and the other standing lookout. I was usually the lookout because I immediately found that I was no great hand at starting the siphon. The gasoline trickled down my throat, causing me to gag and retch noisily, and noise was something to avoid during a siphoning operation. If you had a date that night, it was always best to drop off the girls before you took out the siphoning equipment because your breath wasn't exactly kissing sweet after sucking gas through a rubber hose. It was also advisable not to smoke cigarettes for awhile.

I wouldn't recommend these ideas now. Except one. Talk your girlfriend (or wife) into going parking instead of driving over to Wal-Mart. It's a lot cheaper.

∞⟩⟨∞

REMEMBERING ROAD RAGE

I was driving down US-41, heading for a nice, leisurely lunch at Peggy Sue's Café in Ishpeming. The sun was shining, birds were chirping, soothing classical music drifted from the car radio. I was at peace with the world, cruising along at 55 miles per hour, following the car in front of me at a safe, respectable distance.

Suddenly a monster SUV pulling a trailered boat passed and darted in front of me, the boat missing my front bumper by a scant two feet.

"What the *!!@# are you doing, you ##^&**!!" Cursing wildly, I was about to stomp the Subaru into passing gear, go around the idiot, and do the same thing to him when I stopped in mid "#^%@@!"

I was experiencing road rage.

I carefully unclenched the steering wheel, took a deep breath, slowed, and let the SUV pull away. That was terrible. Not the near miss but the fact that my carefully nurtured veneer of U.P. civility could so easily be shattered. For a few seconds a time warp had zapped me back onto the Los Angeles freeways.

Years ago in Los Angeles I was a daily practitioner of road rage. It wasn't just me. California drivers have developed road rage into an art form. Freeway commuters have mastered the language, facial expressions, using the horn, hand signals involving the middle finger, and, most importantly, how to maneuver their vehicles. For example, traveling up a freeway on-ramp you kick it up to seventy to merge into the traffic in the slow lane. Of course, the slow-lane drivers have no intention of letting you in because it's against California driving protocol. So it becomes a game of chicken. You select the driver you want to cut in front of, give him a I've-got-nothing-to-lose scowl to create indecision in his mind, and then make your move. The faked-out driver swears at you and leans on his horn. With your right hand you flip him the bird so he can see it through your rear window. All standard California road-rage procedure.

Ironically, the maneuver that the SUV pulled on me the other day on US-41 was my own specialty in the old days. On the freeways I could slip into an opening between cars in the next lane that was maybe two inches longer than my vehicle. Unfortunately, while the California Highway Patrol rarely hands out speeding tickets since they want the traffic to keep moving, they took a dim view of my driving habits. In 1970 I got three tickets for "Unsafe Lane Changing," which was patently ridiculous because there was nothing unsafe about my lane changes. I was an expert at it.

But three moving violations in twelve months was going to crank my car insurance up into the stratosphere. So, when the authorities offered me an option to work one of the tickets off my record, I took it. I went to California Highway Patrol driving school.

The driving school was held one night a week for six weeks in a college classroom in the San Fernando Valley. As soon as I walked into class that first evening, I knew I was in the presence of the superstars of traffic scofflaws and road ragers. Among the "students" was a sinister collection of Hell's Angels wannabees, East LA low riders, Crips, Bloods, and other assorted LA gang members. These were not people that you wanted to run into on the roadways after the sun went down, or BEFORE the sun went down, for that matter.

The purpose of the class was to reacquaint us with the California traffic laws which we were so obviously ignoring. It was being taught by an off-duty CHP officer who knew several of the "students" for the simple reason that they'd attended his class before. Included among the traffic rules in the presentation material were slides of horrific accidents with the victims and their living-color innards strewn about the roadway. These scenes, of course, were designed to shock us into safe and sane driving, but they had little effect on the hard-core audience. They had seen them before. "When ya gonna change the pictures?" one leather-clad biker called out.

By far the most exciting part of the class was when it was dismissed. With a crescendo of leather boots, everyone thundered out to the parking lot and jumped into or on their vehicles. Powerful multi-carb engines roared to life, blowing high-octane-fuel exhaust through straight pipes. Everyone rocketed toward the one-lane parking-lot exit in order to be the first to get out. Sparks from low-rider vehicles and burning rubber billowed into the night air, followed by screeching brakes and loud obscenities as they all converged at the exit. The "students" were back in their element. I waited until the air cleared before I even started my engine.

One road-rage incident that I witnessed in 1996 contributed to my decision to move back here. I had just gotten out of my Oldsmobile in a Marina del Rey shopping center when two cars, one chasing the other, came speeding into the parking lot and screeched to a stop. The pursuing driver jumped out of his car with clenched fists and marched toward the other car. The chasee got out of his car, holding a briefcase. He tore open the briefcase and stuck his hand inside as he faced his pursuer. Seeing this, the other guy stepped back to his car, got his own briefcase and also stuck his hand inside. They stood facing each other, hands hidden in their briefcases.

Right about then onlookers began ducking down behind parked cars. I squatted behind my Oldsmobile, convinced that I was about to witness the Gunfight at the Marina del Rey Corral.

After several long seconds both guys backed away and got in their automobiles without flashing any handguns. As they drove away, I stood up, thinking, Do I really want to keep living here? A few months later I was packing up, headed for the U.P.

ഇരു

BRING BACK THE OLD SCHOOL

I get a lot of email—mostly SPAM—but every once in a while I see one worth passing on. My cousin Karen sent me this one.

It seems that the school and teachers at a California high school were being sued by parents who wanted their children's failing grades changed to passing grades even though those teens were absent 15-30 times during the semester and did not complete enough school work to satisfy requirements. The email contains the following message that the high-school office staff supposedly voted to put on the school answering machine.

Hello! You have reached the automated answering service for your school. In order to assist you in connecting to the right staff member, please listen to the following options before making a selection.

To lie about why your child is absent - Press 1.

To make excuses why your child did not do his or her work - Press 2.

To complain about what we do - Press 3.

To swear at staff members - Press 4.

To ask why you didn't get information that was already enclosed in your newsletter and flyers mailed to you - Press 5.

If you want us to raise your child - Press 6.

If you want to reach out and slap someone - Press 7.

To request another teacher for the 3rd time - Press 8.

To complain about our bus transportation - Press 9.

If you realize that this is the real world and your child must be held accountable/responsible for his or her behavior, class work, homework, and that it's not the teacher's fault for your child's lack of effort, hang up and have a nice day.

Of course, this piece is meant to be amusing, but the fact that the lawsuit really happened chills my blood.

Sixty years ago if someone had suggested that my father bring a lawsuit against Central School in Ishpeming in order to get my grades improved, the old man would have said, "Whut th'hell you talkin' about?" No attorney in Ishpeming would have touched the case anyway.

When I was a kid, as soon as you entered the school door, your butt belonged to the school until they let you go in late afternoon. If you behaved in class and paid attention, then everything was fine, but if you wanted to act ugly, then the teachers knew how to play by those rules, too. More than once I got my fingers ruler-whacked by the first-grade teacher at Central whenever I began to get cute with my Palmer ovals. One time in the third grade, for some long-forgotten misdemeanor, I was yanked out of my seat by the hair by Mrs. O'Neill and dragged over to the supply closet where I had to spend an hour of dark solitary confinement.

Republic High School wasn't any easier. The principal, Chet Brown, had some experience with boxing, and would readily snap out a left jab to the nose of any kid he caught smoking in the boy's toilet. Truancy was something else Brown didn't tolerate. One spring afternoon in 1950 a bunch of us boys played hookey to play baseball. Brown got in his car and came looking for us. When he spotted me driving some of the ballplayers home in my Model A, he began chasing us with murder in his heart. We finally eluded him by ditching my car and running into a cedar swamp. However, he was waiting for us at school the next morning. Fortunately, he had cooled off by then and didn't punch us out, but all of the hookey players spent six weeks after school remodelling the school's wood shop.

Aside from the physical punishment handed out by the teachers, there was another excellent incentive for learning. If you didn't cut the mustard during the school year, you didn't advance to the next grade in the fall. You stayed behind. I don't know when the schools abandoned that concept because it certainly worked. It could get rather embarrassing if you had to shave before you went to your fourth-grade class in the morning.

But you know what? It may have taken fourteen years, but when you graduated from high school you knew how to read and write and add, subtract, multiply, and divide. I get the distinct impression that if computers were taken away from today's kids they couldn't make change for a dollar. And one of the most important things that we left school with was a healthy respect for authority, which obviously must be in a state of severe and rapid decline out in California.

I think it would be great if we could somehow bring back the rules of the old schools. Make the parents sign a contract at the beginning of the school year containing the following points written in strict legal language.

• You (parents) will agree to the teachers using any necessary physical discipline to quell disturbances initiated by your child.

• If your child is absent and the school does not receive a call from you stating the reason for the absence, truant officers will initiate a search to bring the child into custody.

• If your child does not perform up to the minimum scholastic standards for his/her grade, then he/she will be held back to repeat the grade next year.

•   You will surrender all rights to bring legal action against the school and its staff for exercising the aforementioned measures.

What do you think? Does this have any chance of becoming a reality something in the future?
I don't think so either.

ஐᏆ

CAMPUS LIFE IN THE VIRTUOUS FIFTIES

An article in a recent USA Today led off with the following sentence: Coming this fall to colleges and universities nationwide: gender-neutral housing.

The crux of the article was that several universities will now have student housing available where members of the opposite sex—and they don't even have to be close friends—can live together in a room or suite and share either a private or a communal bathroom.

Dorm life at today's colleges is apparently light years down the road from when I attended the University of Michigan. Everyone's heard of the Gay Nineties and the Roaring Twenties, right? Well, I was at the U of M during the Virtuous Fifties—that exciting decade when movies contained no foul language, hemlines on women's skirts were below mid-calf, and everybody's underwear was white. Mothers of coed freshmen were assured by U of M officials that their daughter's chastity would remain perfectly intact during their stay at the university. And these weren't just empty promises. All of the women's dormitories, sororities, and co-op houses operated under a strict curfew. Girls had to be safely back in their residence by 10PM or face being put on report. If a coed collected enough of those violations, she was classified as a "loose woman" and asked to leave the university. A guy picking up his date had to wait in a neutral zone on the first floor of the residence under the watchful eye of a housemother. Any man caught on an upper floor of a woman's residence was subject to immediate arrest by the Ann Arbor police.

Men didn't have curfews, but my dormitory also had a house-mother, a hatchet-faced, middle-age matron who kept a constant watch on the stairway to make sure we didn't smuggle women up to our rooms.

During my upperclassman years I lived in a co-op house where things were a bit more relaxed, but even then I managed to run afoul of the university morality police. I had the job of house manager during one summer session when we had a few women taking meals at our house. One day I received a call from the Dean of Women requesting that I come to her office and explain why a neighbor look-ing into our window had spotted females sitting in our living room after 9PM. Females sitting in the living room after 9PM? Can you imagine such a carnal scene? Fortunately, I got off with just a strict warning.

Another time during my senior year I was dating Emily, who later became my first wife. One night we were running around some-where and didn't get back to her co-op house by the 10PM curfew. All of the house doors were locked.

"I guess we'll have to ring the doorbell and get Fran to let you in," I muttered. Fran was Emily's housemother.

"No," Emily said. "There's a basement window that's always unlocked. You can climb in there and sneak up to the kitchen back door and let me in." I was quickly learning that this was not Doris Day I was taking out, but that's a whole other story.

We opened the small basement window, and I shinnied in. What Emily hadn't told me was that this was the window where they delivered coal for the furnace. My feet touched the top of the large pile of coal and I started to slip on the loose coal. I tumbled rump over teakettle, executing three neat somersaults before hitting the floor. A roaring avalanche of coal came down on top of me.

Emily poked her head in the basement window. "Hey, hurry up and open the back door. It's cold out here."

Coughing and choking, I scrambled to my feet, scattering coal in all directions as I groped around in the dark for the stairway. I finally found the bannister and stumbled up the stairs. I opened the door to the kitchen just as the kitchen light went on. Housemother Fran was standing there in her bathrobe.

I must have looked like the Creature From The Black Lagoon because Fran let out an involuntary shriek. After a few moments she composed herself and scowled angrily. "Jerry Harju, is that you beneath all that coal dust?"

Fortunately, I'd been on friendly terms with Fran for some time, so after we let Emily in we all had a cup of coffee in the kitchen and nothing came of the incident except that I had to take a long, hot shower.

So, throughout my college years the university more or less successfully controlled the simmering sexuality of its large student body. Yet, on one occasion the pressure went critical, and the lid blew off with interesting results.

On a warm spring evening in 1952, what began as a friendly ribbing session between two groups of guys from rival dorms across the street from one another, quickly transformed into a large, unruly mob.

"To the women's dorms!" somebody yelled. Given a purpose, the mob, now numbering in the thousands, marched down the street toward the women's dormitories. Worried Ann Arbor police—red lights flashing—followed in patrol cars.

Everyone wondered what atrocities these unhinged sex fiends were going to commit. Rampant kissing? Fondling? Worse? Actually, none of those; remember, this was the 1950's. The mob was in quest of women's underwear. The University of Michigan had just given birth to a panty raid, the first of many that spread like wildfire to other colleges and universities around the country.

Were the women outraged when strange men barged into their rooms looking for bras, slips, and panties? Maybe a few, but for many girls the panty raid was the most exciting thing that had ever happened to them. When the mob faltered with uncertainty outside of a women's dorm entrance, the girls leaned out the upper windows, urging the guys on by tossing bras and panties down into the crowd. In fact, many of the coeds, caught up in the mood, defied curfew and began raiding the MEN'S dorms. Hearing that turn of events really upset me because my BVDs weren't exactly in trophy condition.

But the next day everyone got up and trudged off to class as usual. Women's curfews were back in place. Grim-faced housemothers once again stood guard at dormitory doors. Students had successfully let off steam, and things were back to normal. For this reason, many thought that the panty raid was a good thing.

But how about today's students living in their gender-neutral housing? Guys certainly aren't going to get excited about women's underwear when they have to brush aside drying brassieres in order to shave in the bathroom mirror. How will THEY blow off steam?

Hmmm . . . maybe I don't want to know.

₨₧

A CANDIDATE FOR OUTSOURCING

These days there's a lot of concern over U.S. firms outsourcing jobs to foreign countries like India, China, and Malaysia where labor is cheap. During this election year it's a big bone of contention between Republicans and Democrats. The Democrats raise the point that outsourcing has resulted in millions of U.S. jobs being lost. The Republicans counter with the claim that outsourcing is strengthening the world economy. A stronger world economy will result in lowering the trade deficit because revitalized nations like India and China can now afford to buy our goods. My response is this: what goods are these revitalized countries going to buy from us after we've outsourced all of our manufacturing capability to them? And no, we can't sell them Big Macs. They're already making Big Macs in the third-world countries.

Manufacturing has been outsourced abroad for decades. My khakis are made in China. My shirts come from Guatemala, India, Costa Rica, and Sri Lanka. My favorite Green Bay Packers shirt was made in Bangladesh. And more recently, service jobs and even white-collar positions are being sent overseas. For example, if you're on the phone with an operator of your long-distance carrier, the chances are that the polite lady on the other end of the line is not in Detroit or Chicago but in Calcutta. It's been rumored—and probably true—that job-training firms in India teach applicants how to speak English with a Midwestern twang to put their telephone customers at ease. And it's a good possibility that your PC software has been developed in Asia. U.S. companies are now frequently employing overseas accounting firms to do their bookkeeping for low fees.

But what can we do? We're living in a capitalistic society, so whatever companies can do to legally lower their costs is justifiable and legitimate.

I say, go with the flow. Consider this. We, the American people, are like management of a very large company. We invest capital (our taxes) which is used to pay employees who produce goods and services. So, think a minute. Do you know of any of our employees who are overpaid? Are any overspending our federal funds to get their job done? Do any have overly generous fringe benefits? Uh-huh, you've got it. Let's outsource the job of the President of the United States.

Congress would instantly support the idea, since most congresspersons have trouble getting along with the President for one reason or another. The appropriate constitutional amendments would be passed, and a new president would be found in a country like, say India. Our outgoing President would be treated as fairly as any other downsized employee. He would receive severance pay, and after the appropriate waiting period, he would be eligible for $240 a week unemployment insurance for 13 weeks.

The new President would get a salary of $300 a month, which would not include benefits but would easily be adequate compensation in his country of residence. Due to the time difference between his country and the U.S., the President will work nights, but that will allow him to keep his day job driving a taxi.

To save even more, the entire White House staff would be let go. The Federal Government could get hefty rent for the now-empty White House since any wealthy Washingtonian would snap it up because of its prime location. But before the new tenant moves in, the Federal Government could hold a garage sale on the White House lawn. The fancy furniture, oil paintings, not to mention the White House dinnerware, should fetch a pretty penny.

I'm sure the government could also sell Air Force One, probably to Bill Gates. Bill could use the aircraft to buzz over to his new summer retreat, Camp David.

So you can see that outsourcing the President would save millions and millions of dollars, even billions if we take it one step further and also outsource the Vice President and the Cabinet members. This money could be put to a variety of good uses: hiring more and better teachers, training more nurses, better health care for the elderly, and repairing our roads.

Speaking of roads, I can think of one U.P. job that will never be in danger of being outsourced.

Patching potholes.

ଛୁଓଃ

YOUNG OPINIONS ON LOVE

Valentine's Day is approaching, so it's a good time to talk about love, the opposite sex, marriage, and all that stuff. Do you remember when you were a kid and these exotic topics were nibbling at your mind? I do. Over the years several famous people have asked children about their thoughts on love, and I've collected some of the answers. These are all factual responses. I could never have made them up.

WHY DOES LOVE HAPPEN BETWEEN TWO PEOPLE?
"I think you get shot with an arrow or something, but the rest of it isn't supposed to be so painful." Harlen, 8 years old.
"No one is sure why it happens, but I heard it has something to do with how you smell. That's why perfume and deodorant are so popular." Jan, 9 years old.

WHAT IS FALLING IN LOVE LIKE?
"If falling in love is anything like learning how to spell, I don't want to do it. It takes too long." Leo, 7 years old.
"Like an avalanche where you have to run for your life." Roger, 9 years old.

WHAT EFFECT DO GOOD LOOKS HAVE ON LOVE?

"If you want to be loved by somebody who isn't already in your family, it doesn't hurt to be beautiful." Jeanne, 8 years old.

"It isn't always just how you look. Look at me, I'm handsome like anything, and I haven't got anybody to marry me yet." Gary, 7 years old.

"Beauty is skin deep. But how rich you are can last a long time." Christine, 9 years old.

WHY DO LOVERS HOLD HANDS?

"They want to make sure their rings don't fall off, because they paid good money for them." Dave, 8 years old.

HOW DO YOU MAKE SOMEONE FALL IN LOVE WITH YOU?

"Don't do things like have smelly, green sneakers. You might get attention, but attention ain't the same thing as love." Alonzo, 9 years old.

"One way is to take the girl out to eat. Make sure it's something she likes to eat. French fries usually work for me." Bart, 9 years old.

HOW DO YOU MAKE LOVE LAST?

"Spend most of your time loving instead of going to work." Tom, 7 years old.

"Be a good kisser. It might make your wife forget that you never take out the trash." Randy, 8 years old.

WHEN IS IT OKAY TO KISS SOMEONE?

"You should never kiss a girl unless you have enough bucks to buy her a big ring and her own VCR, because she'll want to have videos of the wedding." Jim, 10 years old.

"Never kiss in front of other people. It's a big embarrassing thing if anybody sees you. But if nobody sees you, I might be willing to try it with a handsome boy, but just for a few hours." Kally, 9 years old.

"It's never okay to kiss a boy. They always slobber all over you. That's why I stopped doing it." Jean, 10 years old.

WHAT ARE MOST PEOPLE THINKING WHEN THEY SAY "I LOVE YOU"?

"The person is thinking, 'Yeah, I really do love him. But I hope he showers at least once a day." Michelle, 9 years old.

HOW CAN YOU TELL IF TWO ADULTS EATING DINNER AT A RESTAURANT ARE IN LOVE?

"Just see if the man picks up the check. That's how you can tell if he's in love." John, 9 years old.

IS IT BETTER TO BE SINGLE OR MARRIED?

"It gives me a headache to think about that stuff. I'm just a kid. I don't need that kind of trouble." Kenny, 7 years old.

WHAT QUALITIES ARE NECESSARY IN A GOOD MATE?

"One of you should know how a write a check. Because even if you have tons of love, there is still going to be a lot of bills." Ava, 8 years old.

WHAT IS THE PROPER AGE TO GET MARRIED?

"Eighty-four, because at that age, you don't have to work any more, and you can spend all your time loving each other in the bedroom." Judy, 8 years old.

"Once I'm done with kindergarten, I'm going to find me a wife." Tom, 5 years old.

WHAT IS IT ABOUT YOU THAT MAKES WOMEN WANT YOU?
"My ears. They're big, and I can wiggle them." Jack, 10 years old.

WHAT DO YOU THINK OF LOVE?
"I'm in favor of love as long as it doesn't happen when 'The Simpsons' is on television." Anita, 6 years old.

WHAT'S YOUR IDEA OF THE PERFECT GIRL?
"There aren't any." Brian, 8 years old.

WHAT'S THE NICEST THING A BOY HAS EVER DONE FOR YOU?
"He moved." Lisa, 10 years old.

80CR

OUR GOVERNMENT IN TODAY'S TOYLAND

The Consumer Product Safety Commission (CPSC) is a government watchdog that monitors every piece of merchandise you buy to make sure you don't kill or maim yourself with it when you get it home. They require manufacturers to attach warning labels to products to avoid misuse or accidents. Interestingly, some of these warnings are the result of—dare I use the word "frivolous"?—lawsuits. For example, there are now take-out coffee cups at some fast-food places that warn: CAUTION: THE CONTENTS OF THIS CONTAINER ARE HOT AND CAN CAUSE BURNS.

The CPSC has really had an impact on toy manufacturing. Toys are now mostly made of smooth molded plastic with no sharp edges on which a child could cut himself and no small pieces that could be swallowed. Toys are plastered with warning labels, like: CAUTION: IF THIS TOY BECOMES BROKEN, DISCARD IT IMMEDIATELY. If that rule was in place when I was a kid, we would have been without toys. Every kid I knew played with broken toys. We had no other kind.

You don't even see balloons in toy departments anymore because they can be a choking hazard if a child inadvertently breathes in when he should be blowing out. Cords on pull toys should be no longer than twelve inches so they can't be tangled into a dangerous loop.

The CPSC strongly suggests that all toy guns should be brightly colored so they won't be mistaken for a real gun that someone could use in a liquor-store holdup. I don't go along with that. Robbers get plenty of real guns at cheap prices, and little boys all want one that looks like the real thing. Who needs a pink pistol.

Many of the toys we had in the 1940's would never have passed muster with the Consumer Product Safety Commission. For example, there were plenty of realistic-looking toy guns for sale, and some fired real ammunition of sorts. One popular item was a black, spring-loaded toy revolver that shot a six-inch-long wooden rod with a rubber suction cup on one end. The suction cup was supposed to stick to a paper target. I got one of those for Christmas one year. After shooting at the target a few times I got bored with that, so what do you suppose I did? Why, I took off the rubber suction cup, of course! With my new Christmas jackknife—which also wouldn't be on the CPSC's approved list—I whittled one end of the rod to a sharp point, loaded the pistol, and went outside, looking for some Catholic kid I had it in for.

Water pistols were also popular when I was a kid. The neat thing about water pistols was that they'd fire any kind of fluid. (You probably know where I'm headed with this.) One summer, during a heated water-pistol war, we'd first stand over the toilet in the bathroom, fill up a mason jar, and then carry it outside and load up our pistols. You'd run up to an adversary, take careful aim, and BAM! right in the kisser. (Could that be why the Consumer Product Safety Commission doesn't approve of water pistols?)

Another thing you don't see anymore are wood-burning kits. It had a soldering-iron type of tool that you'd plug in and the metal tip would heat up to about 5000 degrees. Pressing the hot tip into a wooden board, you could burn in your name or even draw a picture if you had artistic talent. Some kids found other uses. One boy in

South Ishpeming was playing cowboy in his bedroom and thought it would be neat to brand his sister's cat with a lazy S. It didn't work out. With one swipe of her claws, the cat branded him first.

I remember the Christmas I got my Gilbert chemistry set, a large metal box filled with beakers, various instruments, and many mysterious substances in bottles and cans. It also had a small Bunsen burner to heat up your concoctions to a boil. It came with a book of directions so you could make magic substances to amaze your friends and family.

And what do you suppose was the first thing I wanted to do with my chemistry set?

Why, build a bomb, of course!

And in the Gilberts book they actually had a recipe for making an explosive, complete with directions for fashioning a fuse to blow it up. (Can you imagine what the Consumer Product Safety Commission would say about that?)

I hustled up to my bedroom with my new chemistry set and busily mixed up the compounds for the explosive. Then I dipped store string into the fuse mixture. I lit the string and it burned nicely right up to the explosive. I stuck my fingers in my ears.

The explosive powder made a wimpy little POP and disappeared in a tiny cloud of smoke. My mother downstairs in the kitchen didn't even hear it. I didn't play much with that dumb chemistry set after that.

Seriously though, the Consumer Products Safety Commission has done a splendid job keeping toys safe for children and over the years has been responsible for preventing injuries and saving lives. Now if they could just do something about the loud music the kids listen to. It can't be doing their ears much good.

‑‑‑

I'M AN ALL-WHEEL-DRIVER NOW

I was born in the U.P., but after getting an engineering degree at the University of Michigan I wound up in California with a job in the aerospace business. I stayed out there for thirty-eight years. After taking early retirement I moved back to the U.P. in 1996, just in time for a record snowy winter. I had to get reacquainted with snow.

My California Oldsmobile—a two-wheel, rear drive— didn't like the U.P. winter one bit. It couldn't seem to stop at intersections, and took me into several heart-stopping spins. The retractable radio antenna sampled the frigid air a few times, retreated back into the fender well, and never came out again. The electric windows stopped going down.

I bought a Chevy Lumina which was a fine car, but it didn't like deep snow either. I kept getting stuck in my apartment parking area and even succeeded in bashing it into the center divider on US-41 when I lost control in the snow. Then I purchased a new Buick LeSabre which is such an elegant car that I'm afraid to drive it in the winter so I keep it in the garage.

This time of year whenever I get together with folks, I'm the only one talking about spin-outs and getting stuck. They smile tolerantly when I tell them about my near disasters on slippery roadways because they all own four-wheel-drives.

It finally dawned on me that if I was going to die in bed, which has been my plan all along, I'd better get a four-wheel drive vehicle.

I shopped around and finally settled on a Subaru Outback. The unique feature of the Subaru is All-Wheel-Drive (AWD). The Subaru people claim that AWD is vastly superior to four-wheel-drive because it's smarter, using an electronically managed continuously variable transfer clutch that anticipates wheel slippage and transfers power to the front or rear wheels with the best traction, even before slippage occurs. (If any of you mechanical geniuses out there understand this, drop me a line. I wasn't that kind of engineer.)

Not only does my Outback have AWD, it's got plenty of other fancy stuff. I've got electronically heated seats! You just climb in on a cold morning, flip a switch, and in less than a minute your buns are nice and toasty.

When I first moved back here in '96 I laughed when my friend Jeff told me that he had heated rear-view side mirrors on his Jeep Cherokee. "What in the world are heated mirrors good for?" I asked. Now I've got them on my Subaru, and boy, are they neat. The ice just runs off of them. (Californians wouldn't have the foggiest idea what a heated rear-view mirror is.)

But, of course, the thing I really like about the Subaru is the way it runs through deep snow. A brainy computer somewhere deep in the bowels of this machine directs each wheel to reach out and grab the snow for all it's worth. It's like the tires have claws—they don't spin.

The day before I bought the Outback I was out test-driving it, and Deb Danielson at Crown Motors was kind enough to let me take it home overnight. It began to snow and snowed all night into the morning. I looked out my bedroom window, and my heart began pumping excitedly. Deep snow! I couldn't get into my clothes fast enough. Chuckling to myself I tromped through the snow, brushed off the Outback, got in and started it up. I turned on my heated seat and mirrors and headed for the street.

The plows hadn't gotten to my neighborhood yet, and there was a good six inches of fresh snow on Arch Street. "Good, good!" I chortled to myself as I foraged through the snow toward downtown Marquette.

The snow was still coming down like crazy, and I zigzagged through town, looking for near-impassible streets and steep, slippery hills. My new vehicle took it all in stride, and I lovingly patted the steering wheel. No more spin-outs! No more shoveling axle-deep snow away from the wheels.!

"I need more snow and ice!" I shouted at astounded motorists at red lights.

I drove up to Crown Motors to close the deal. They hadn't had a chance to plow their parking lot yet. I loved it. I parked the Outback in the deepest snow I could find on the lot and went inside with my checkbook.

It's now the next day, and I'm sad to say that the snow has stopped, and all of the streets have been plowed, salted, and sanded. But I'm not done. The plows have created big snowbanks, so I'm going out to find some whoppers to drive through.

ଏଡାର

THIS AIN'T FISHIN' FOR FUN

When I first took up fishing as a kid, my equipment was primitive–a long branch cut from a poplar tree with a piece of fish line tied to one end. A sinker and hook with a worm on it and I was in business. Eventually, I ordered an honest-to-gawd fishing pole and reel from the Montgomery Ward catalog. The pole cost $1.75 and the reel about the same. That fishing gear was all I needed for a long time.

I bring this up because I was recently introduced to fishing that's sixteen light years out from my early angling experiences. Jim Muffler is a hair stylist in Marquette, but that's not his real passion. Jim's a bass fisherman. I don't mean that he sits in a small boat with a six-pack of beer on a Sunday afternoon, hoping to get lucky. Uh-uh. Muffler enters sanctioned bass tournaments, angling for big prize money. In fact, Jim Muffler is one of the top bass fishermen in Upper Michigan.

During one of my haircuts Jim invited me to go along on a practice fishing run before an upcoming weekend bass tournament. Smelling an interesting column, I readily agreed.

Late Friday afternoon I joined Jim at the Greenwood Reservoir south of Ishpeming. He backed his trailered fishing boat down to the water and launched it. I use the term "fishing boat" loosely because this boat resembles something used to outrun the Coast Guard while smuggling dope in from South America. The fiberglass hull on the Allison XB-2002 is designed to basically hydroplane above the water, not too difficult since mounted on the aft end was the biggest monster outboard engine I'd ever seen. This thing—a Mercury 280HP—was bigger than my Buick, not the engine, the WHOLE Buick.

Muffler explained that this is your basic bass boat. If you're wondering why a bass angler needs a boat that could run down a cruise missile, it's because in a bass tournament you have to catch the most and biggest fish in an allotted period of time. The bodies of water are large, and the fishermen have scouted out several likely bass hangouts, often several miles apart. They can't waste precious time loafing along enjoying the scenery, so they need a boat with lots of zip. After all, this is not some trivial fun sport.

I gingerly stepped into the boat. "Wow! Some rig. It looks like it'd go about a hundred miles an hour."

"It WILL go a hundred miles an hour," Jim said.

I sat down in the aft bucket seat. Jim handed me a life jacket which I quickly buckled on. There were no seat belts, the reasoning being that in case of an accident in a speeding bass boat the last thing you want is to be attached to the boat.

The boat had more equipment on it than the Space Shuttle. The pilot's control console had the usual instrumentation found on any automobile, but in addition there was a hi-tech big-screen sonar/GPS unit providing depth contour displays, fish finding, and waterway mapping to any desired magnification. Jim inserted a chip into the unit which contained an entire map of the U.P. Within seconds he brought up a detailed display of the Greenwood Reservoir. Big-time bass fishermen conduct a preliminary reconnaissance of the tournament waters, noting likely bass spots. These locations are punched into the GPS unit which records them on an electronic map. The next morning the GPS provides navigation vectors, directly guiding the angler back to the good spots. It must be eerie fishing from a boat that's smarter than you are.

On the bow of bass boats is an electric trolling motor steered by two foot pedals on the deck. The fisherman stands on the bow, making casts, using his feet to maneuver the boat at trolling speed. Within easy reach are his array of poles, fastened to the bow deck with velcro straps. In a bass tournament no one wastes time switching lures on the line if one isn't working. They simply grab another pole. Jim had five poles strapped to the deck, all rigged with different lures with names like: Yamamoto Senko, jig skirts, brush hogs, hula grubs, and crankbaits.

Among the various storage compartments on board are fish tanks called livewells. No bass dies during a tournament; they're kept alive in the livewell, weighed at the end of the day, and then released. In fact, if a bass in the livewell dies accidently before it's weighed, the angler is disqualified. So if you're motoring in to shore with a prize bass and the fish begins looking peaked, you'd better give it mouth-to-mouth resuscitation, which is not easy with a large-mouth bass.

Jim started up the huge Mercury engine and turned to me. "We're set to go."

"Let 'er rip," I said.

"Hang on to your hat."

The engine bellowed out an ugly roar, and the bass boat leapt out of the water and rocketed away from the dock. My right hand pinned my Tilley sun hat to the back of my head while my left kept a death grip on a cockpit safety handle. The front brim of the hat plastered itself over my eyes, rendering me sightless, which was probably just as well. Ninety seconds later, when Jim slowed the boat enough to allow me to see again, we were almost two miles from the dock. "I didn't open it up all the way," Muffler commented. "Maybe just a li'l over eighty."

He immediately set about doing some serious bass fishing, grabbing one pole after another, casting baits into thickets of dead branches and stumps close to shore. The pace was frantic, Muffler making four or five casts a minute, selecting a variety of spots he wanted to drop the bait. I quickly found that a vital bassmaster skill is accurate casting. Jim could drop a bait into your coffee cup at forty feet. He had several strikes, convincing himself he knew where to begin fishing the next morning.

On Sunday afternoon I went to the reservoir to observe the final weigh-in. Muffler didn't win the tournament this time, but on both days he'd had gotten his limit of nice-size bass.

Maybe one day we'll see Jim Muffler's picture on a Wheaties box.

ଞଠଶ

DUMB LIQUOR LAWS

Some weeks ago my friend Jeff, my cousin Karen, and I went down to Wisconsin to see the Whistling Straits golf course where the PGA championship had recently been held. That evening we went to an upscale restaurant in Sheboygan for dinner. A polite young man took our dinner orders and also our order for wine to go with the meal. He reappeared shortly with the bottle of wine on a tray.

Somewhat embarrassed, he said to me, "Could you please take the wine from the tray and put it on the table?"

I looked at him questioningly and he explained. "I'm only sixteen, and I'm not allowed to handle containers of alcoholic beverages."

It seems that Wisconsin restaurants with liquor licenses—and this may be true in other states as well—can employ underage servers as long as the "kids" don't handle the drink containers. The bartender places beer, wine, and mixed drinks on the server's tray, and the customers at the table have the job to lift them off.

That got the three of us talking about dumb liquor laws, dumb because these laws on the books of various states and Canada—many dating back to Puritan times—do little if anything to regiment or discourage drinking.

Karen, who lives near Houston, told us about a peculiar rule in some Texas counties. It's illegal for a bar or restaurant to sell you a mixed drink, but they'll sell you a glass filled with ice cubes and 7-UP, Coke, or whatever you want—called a "setup"—and you furnish the booze and mix your own. You bring a bottle of whiskey, vodka, or whatever into the place in a paper bag and pour a shot, or two, or three into the setup glass and down the hatch. You can get drunk out of your gourd sitting there, and the establishment can't regulate how much you drink because it's your liquor. What that law is supposed to accomplish, I have no idea.

Canada has had some of my favorite dumb liquor laws. In 1975 two friends and I were exploring Canada's Northwest Territory. One Sunday afternoon we set up camp at a small remote outpost on the McKenzie River. We went into the restaurant/bar and ordered beers. The lone waitress explained that since it was Sunday we could only get alcoholic beverages if we also ordered food, the idea being, I suppose, that the government didn't want anyone getting drunk on Sunday, and food keeps you sober.

That was fine, we said, we were going to eat anyway. So we ordered food from the menu and got our beer.

Two bewhiskered men in dirty plaid shirts—obviously locals—lumbered in and sat down at a nearby table. The waitress wordlessly put a shot of whiskey and a beer in front of each of them. By the time we got our food, these two were working on their third round of drinks.

Through some unspoken understanding, the waitress brought two steaming plates of food to the drinkers. Hot turkey sandwiches, heaps of mashed potatoes, string beans, all swimming in gravy. She also placed a paper shopping bag lined with waxed paper on the floor between their chairs and then went back to the kitchen.

The two locals tipped their plates over the bag, slopping in the contents and then resumed drinking. They'd eat the food later, but no goofy law was going to keep them from their current mission of getting drunk.

Some of these laws enacted to reduce drinking actually have the reverse effect. When I was a senior at the University of Michigan in 1956 I spent spring break with a Canadian friend of mine, Jim Hunter, at his home in Toronto. One afternoon Hunter introduced me to a Canadian beer parlor. These places were called "dime stores" because all they sold were dime glasses of beer. The place was packed. Sturdily built waitresses circulated among the crowd, balancing huge trays filled with glasses of beer on one hand.

Jim went up to a cashier and got ten dimes for a dollar bill. We sat down at an empty table, and Hunter put the dimes on the table. Within three seconds a waitress slapped two beers down and whisked away two of the dimes.

As I was sipping my beer I noticed that everyone else, including Jim, were drinking theirs at a pretty good clip. As soon as customers finished their beer, they'd bang the empty glass on the table. A waitress would immediately scoop up the empty and a dime with one hand and put down a fresh beer with the other.

It seems that the Canadians, at least in Toronto, had a law prohibiting customers from having more than one drink in front of them at any given time. This was designed to keep patrons from drinking too much. However, the pub owners didn't want customers suffering from thirst between drinks, so they provided extremely fast service. If a beer drinker didn't get a refill within five seconds after banging his empty glass on the table, he was entitled to shout, "Hey, how about a little service here!" Within seconds a full glass would be slammed down in front of him.

Over time this evolved into a sport. Who was faster, the customers or the servers? Everyone including the pub owners loved it, and the pace became lightning quick with practice. The banging of empty and full beer glasses on the tables sounded like an army of berserk flamenco dancers. Customers were getting boggley-eyed drunk in twenty minutes. The law originally intended to prevent folks from drinking too much had the opposite result.

Why haven't state and local governments tried education instead of enacting these idiotic liquor laws, which never seem to work? Teach kids while they're still in school about the consequences of alcohol abuse. Don't pull any punches. Show them a color picture of a cirrhotic liver taken from the cadaver of an alcoholic. Better yet, make them spend Saturday night—cold sober, of course—in the drunk tank of the city jail. That'll get their attention.

ഇൻ

LIVING IN "PARADISE"

For years I've listened to people up here complaining that if they could only afford it, they'd move to Florida. They're sick and tired of cold and snow and want to relocate to the Sunshine State where balmy breezes blow and serene beaches beckon to you from just beyond your front door.

Well, if you've been watching CNN lately, you know that those balmy Florida breezes have been clipping along smartly at one-hundred-plus miles an hour, and the serene beaches have been sucked into the sea by fierce storm surges. Nobody knows for sure where the front door went. It was last seen heading west at an altitude of three hundred feet.

After four hurricanes smashed across the state in six weeks, Florida has become the world's biggest junkyard, totally covered with twisted aluminum siding, downed power lines, chunks of mobile homes, and beached yachts. It'll take months to clean up the mess.

But just watch, by January the hurricanes will be long forgotten, and the "snowbirds" will once again be flocking to Florida on their annual migration from New York, New England, and the Midwest to warm their feathers in the southern sun.

I can understand why snowbirds like to spend a few winter months in Florida, but what really baffles me is why people move there permanently. I've been in Florida several times, and the winter warmth is about the only thing it's got going for it.

For one thing, Florida is the flattest state in the Union. That's right, even flatter than pool-table North Dakota. The highest point in Florida is 345 feet. They probably call it Mount something or other. Actually, Florida is a paved swamp. The whole state smells like decaying vegetation. Travel agents like to call it tropical fragrance, but it smells like a swamp to me. In fact, Florida has another nickname besides the Sunshine State. They call it the Alligator State. That's because if the people moved out, within a few years the whole place would be overrun by alligators.

Actually, Florida's alligators are in trouble because their swamps are quickly being absorbed by cookie-cutter pastel condominiums populated with retired people my age or older. I ask you, who wants to associate with herds of geezers like me? Think of the danger. You're crossing the street and a 5000 pound Cadillac driven by a little ninety-year-old person who can't see over the steering wheel is bearing down on you.

Florida maintains one of the highest crime rates in the country. Pickpockets, muggers, car thieves and burglars flock there. Why Florida? Because senior citizens are easy pickings. Transplanted retirees from small towns in Michigan, Wisconsin, Minnesota, and the Dakotas are easy prey because they've spent a lifetime trusting people. But in Florida they quickly learn to get electronic deposits for their Social Security checks, keep a firm grip on their purses and wallets, and not leave the car keys in the ignition. Chaining your walker to your wrist is a good idea because there's a healthy market for them in the Sunshine State.

Oh, and incidently, one last reminder about Florida. Don't forget about the hurricanes.

These same Floridian wannabes come up and ask me why in the world I ever left California. I give them my standard answer: I didn't like the four seasons out there—fire, flood, smog, and riots, not to mention earthquakes, long lines at movie theaters, drug stores, supermarkets, banks, and video stores, and the insufferable freeway traffic. Incidentally, there's no such thing as rush-hour traffic in California anymore; it's now bumper to bumper 24/7.

So, think about it, the winters are warm, but the so-called "paradise" states like Florida and California have lots of downsides.

Right now we're coming into one of the most beautiful seasons of the year in the U.P. when Mother Nature shows us what she can do with her paintbrush. You don't have to drive in heavy traffic to see the fall colors, and it's all free. Okay, so we get a lot of snow in the winter, even blizzards. But when it blows over you don't have to go looking for your roof.

₨₧

HALLOWEEN AROUND THE WORLD

Orange and black decorations dot the landscape and huge stacks of pumpkins line US-41 near the Marquette Mall. Candy makers and dentists are rubbing their hands in glee, because October is the peak season for Reese's Peanut Butter Cups, candy corn, M&M's, and Snickers bars.

It's Halloween, and the merchants love it. Frankenstein, Dracula, and witch costumes have become passe. Kids now want to be Spider Man, Harry Potter, Barbie, and Power Rangers. And every year adults are getting into the act more and more. For you adventurous ladies, Shopko has a sale on Halloween panties with your choice of a strategically placed grinning jack-o-lantern or a large black spider.

I remember Halloween when it wasn't the merchant's golden goose. Costumes were made using mama's dresses and makeup, old bed sheets, or anything else you could scrounge up in the attic, cellar, or woodshed. And back then Trick or Treating had teeth in it. If the people answering the door didn't come up with candy, popcorn balls, or at the very least, an apple, they were prime targets for waxed windows, rocks in their car hubcaps, or burning bags of doggie do-do on the doorstep.

Many people think that Halloween is strictly an American observance. Not true. Halloween didn't even originate in the United States.

Thousands of years ago in Ireland there was a tribe called the Celts. They knew that the sun helped make their crops grow, so when autumn arrived and the sun began to fade they worried that it wouldn't return again. Consequently they held a festival on October 31, during which they asked the sun to come back safely in the summer. Feasts were held around bonfires, and people dressed up in animal skins, believing that these costumes would protect them from bad luck. The Celts also believed that on this date the veil between the worlds of the living and the dead grew thinner, and ghosts ventured toward the warmth of people's homes and hearths. Around the bonfires, in memory of their departed ancestors, the Celts put out food and drink at night for the ghosts. They stayed on good terms with the spirits by getting them mellow.

Centuries passed and in an effort to convert the Celts to Christianity, Pope Gregory III moved All Saints' Day, more commonly known as All Hallows, to 1 November to coincide with the Celts' celebration. The 31 October date then became known as All Hallow' Eve, which eventually was shortened to Halloween.

As time passed Irish children got into the act and began cutting scary faces into hollowed-out turnips, large rutabagas, or potatoes and placing a lit candle inside them. Soon they found that it was more fun to throw the vegetables at people's doors on Halloween. Sound familiar?

Halloween celebrations spread to England. In some areas Halloween was known as "Mischief Night," a night for pranks on which even adults participated. Jokesters would take people's doors off their hinges and throw them into ponds or carry them a long distance away. That sounds familiar too.

There was a strong belief in some British Isle villages that on Halloween night elves rode on the backs of the village cats. Villagers locked up their cats at night to keep the elves off their backs. And here's a switch; black cats were considered to be good luck whereas white cats were bad luck.

When Christianity became dominant in Britain, Halloween fell out of favor because it was considered a pagan festival. Only recently—due to American television—have British kids taken up Halloween Trick or Treating. The problem is that many Brit oldsters have never heard of it. When they see small persons wearing masks on their front doorstep they think it's a home invasion and call the police.

But Halloween commercialism is creeping into Great Britain. Toward the end of October, old castles on the island suddenly and mysteriously become haunted by ghosts of medieval aristocracy, including murdered sixteenth-century children and Anne Boleyn carrying her head under her arm. For a stiff price newlyweds can rent a haunted three-turreted honeymoon suite at the Castle Stuart in Inverness, Scotland. I think I'd pass on that. Marriage is scary enough without adding ghosts.

Most people wouldn't dream of going to a graveyard on Halloween, but in Mexico it's the thing to do. All Saints' Day (1 November) is devoted to Los Angelitos—the dead children. The little ghosts get a head start on grown-up ghosts who arrive in full force the following day. November 2 is Dia de los Muertos, Day of the Dead, a national holiday in Mexico. It's a day of remembrance, happiness, and celebration, and Mexicans have picnics on the graves of their beloved relatives. Housewives make candy in the shapes of skulls, caskets and skeletons. To help the ghosts find their way back home, parents and other family members shoot off firecrackers and often strew a path of flower petals from the graveyard to their front door.

This year I may conduct my own personal Halloween celebration. I'll get a rubber John Kerry mask and go out and scare some Republicans.

∽◯◈

BC (before color) TV

The other day American Furniture in Marquette was having a big sale on TVs. I normally don't pay attention to TV ads, but this one caught my eye. You can now buy a TV with a SEVENTY-INCH screen. SEVENTY INCHES? Something like that in my living room would tie my neck in a knot looking from one side of the picture to the other.

The first TV I ever saw had a screen about 1/100 that size. In the summer of 1949 my parents and I were working and living at a golf and country club outside of Milwaukee. One evening my father excitedly burst into my room.

"Albert just gotta television!" Albert was the club's headwaiter who also lived on the premises.

"What's a television?" I asked.

"C'mon up to his room and take a look."

Albert's room was filled with guys puffing on cigarettes, their eyes glued to a bulky floor-model radio-like console. But the thing had a tiny 6 by 8 inch black and white picture screen. The picture was fuzzy and flickered constantly, but no one cared. There were little people in it, and they were moving around.

I elbowed my way over to the console and looked in the back to figure out where the picture was coming from. All I could see was a tangle of wires, a bunch of vacuum tubes, and a huge alien-looking glass tube.

On top of the console was a pair of long metal rods which I found out later was a rabbit-ear antenna. From time to time one of the viewers trying to get a closer look would brush up against the antenna, sending the picture into a tizzy.

"Don't do that!" Albert would yell. He'd struggle out of his chair and tweak the rabbit ears to get the picture back.

The TV program was a wrestling match, but we watched it like it was game seven of the World Series. From time to time a commercial came on—some guy in downtown Milwaukee selling used cars—and we watched that, too. Albert finally had to kick everyone out so he could go to bed.

Because television was still unknown in the U.P., the next time I saw TV was in 1951 when I went to Ann Arbor as a freshman at the U of M. I lived in a dormitory that had one TV set on the first-floor. The screen was a bit larger than the first one I saw but not much.

The dorm TV always drew a crowd of guys. We could get two Detroit stations, so every half hour a vote had to be taken to decide which channel we'd watch. Early TV sets required constant adjustments, and remote controls were still years away. One of the viewers—usually an electrical-engineering student because they were supposed to know about TV—was the appointed picture technician. He sat near the TV and from time to time would jump up and adjust the horizontal and vertical hold to keep the picture from going cockeyed.

TV wrestling was still a big draw, but now I was exposed to other programming. "Kukla, Fran and Ollie" came on an hour before we marched off to the dining room for dinner and always drew a big audience. The dry wit of Ollie—a green dragon—appealed to us sophisticated college men.

There was a brand new police drama featuring a couple of Los

Angeles detectives. Everyone loved this program because of the realistic, businesslike way these two guys conducted investigations. When interviewing a witness to a crime one of them would say, "Just the facts, ma'am." This, of course, was Jack Webb in "Dragnet," and no one realized that we'd keep hearing that phrase for decades to come.

And on Sunday nights we always tuned in to watch a wooden-faced fellow who had "a really big shew." Ed Sullivan could put on a variety show with talent ranging from Henry Fonda reading Lincoln's Gettysburg Address to a troupe of dancing penguins.

A few years later Elvis Presley's hips made their TV debut on Ed Sullivan's show. Elvis's hot hips came as a big shock to both the viewing public and CBS executives. Remember, '50's TV programs weren't taped. Everything was live. CBS was deluged with outraged calls and letters, and thereafter on Ed Sullivan shows featuring Elvis, the cameras were trained exclusively on his upper body.

In 1965 my wife, Joanne, her son, Greg, and I moved into a house in Hermosa Beach, California. While forking out large sums of money on furniture we also decided to splurge on a color TV. We selected a Magnavox with a huge 19-inch screen, very pricey, but we wanted the best.

The first thing I had to do was put up a TV roof antenna. Because of our low beach-front location, the antenna had to be mounted on a forty-foot mast, held in place on the roof by long sturdy guy wires. The antenna cost as much as the TV set.

Adjusting the picture on color TV was twice as demanding as black and white. In addition to fiddling with the horizontal and vertical holds, you also had knobs for tinting and contrast. We'd be watching "Laugh In" with a teenage Goldie Hawn prancing around in a skimpy bikini, and suddenly her skin would turn green. Ten-year-old Greg had quickly picked up the intricacies of color fine tuning, so it became his job to jump up from the couch and twiddle the knobs.

In 1978 I bought a new TV that came with a little hand-held gizmo covered with buttons. The user's manual called it a remote control. It was interesting because there weren't any buttons on the remote for horizontal and vertical holds or tint and contrast control. Modern TV technology had made these controls unnecessary.

I aimed the remote at the TV and pressed the power button. Presto, the TV came on! Hey, I thought, this is all right. I popped open a can of Diet Fresca, flopped down on the couch, and pressed more buttons, flipping through the channels.

I didn't know it at the time, but I'd just entered the first evolutionary stage of becoming a couch potato.

෨෬

THE LAST DEER HUNT

We're right in the middle of firearm deer season now, the time of year when I stay out of the woods since I don't own a flak jacket. I haven't hunted in over thirty-five years, mainly because I'm not into shooting animals anymore. But there's another reason. The last time I went deer hunting convinced me that I wasn't up to it anymore.

In the late sixties, I lived in Southern California, married to my second wife, Joanne We used to pal around with a couple, Ed and JoAnn Weaver. Ed was an avid hunter, and early one November he asked me if I wanted to go deer hunting. I explained that I hadn't hunted since high school and didn't even own a rifle anymore. Ed said, no problem, he'd lend me one of his. He also confided that he had done some reconnoitering north of Los Angeles and found a spot where we couldn't miss getting our bucks. Fond memories of U.P. deer season flashed before my eyes, and I agreed to go.

A week later my wife and I, camping gear and provisions packed into our tiny Datsun station wagon, followed the Weavers in their camper. The spot Ed had in mind wasn't just north of Los Angeles, it was WAY north—350 miles—high up in the Sierra Nevada Mountains, just east of Yosemite National Park. The Datsun wheezed as we labored up steep grades. At an altitude of over 7000 feet, on any given winter this area can get more snow than Upper Michigan.

Finally, just before dark, we pulled into a campsite on the edge of a mountain stream. Ed and I gathered wood and built a fire while the two women made coffee and brought out food for dinner.

By the time we'd finished eating it was really getting chilly, but I had anticipated the cold and came prepared. Back in those days my wife and I were partial to a hearty beverage called coffee royal, or at least our version of it. Sophisticated people drink café royale—coffee and brandy with sugar and a touch of cinnamon. Our version was simpler—strong black coffee with a slug of Jim Beam whiskey. It did the job just fine.

We threw more wood on the fire, brought out our guitars, and proceeded to serenade any wild critters who cared to listen. It got even colder, but it mattered not because we were fortifying ourselves with plenty of coffee royals.

Finally, we put our guitars up, doused the fire, and called it a night. Deer hunting is really fun, I thought, as Joanne and I happily crawled into sleeping bags in the rear of the station wagon.

The next thing I knew someone was shaking me. Actually, the whole station wagon was shaking. Ed Weaver was playfully bouncing the Datsun up and down to wake me up.

"C'mon, Harju, it's gonna be daylight soon. Gotta get going."

Joanne stuck her head out from her sleeping bag and blearily snarled at me. "Get out, so he'll quit doing that!" The women weren't going deer hunting, so she rolled over and went back to sleep.

For some reason, in my blissful coffee-royal state the night before, I'd decided that it was a good idea to take off my clothes before I crawled into the sleeping bag. I unzipped the bag, crawled out the back end of the Datsun in my skivvies, and immediately turned blue. The temperature was about fifteen degrees, and whereas the air had been fresh and invigorating the night before, that morning it was thin and frigid. I gasped for breath as I hopped around on bare feet looking for my clothes.

The morning after a night of coffee royals always left me with a tremendous thirst. I dug around in our gear, looking for the soft drinks we had packed. I finally found a six-pack of Fresca and frantically tore the tab off of a can and tilted it up to my lips.

Nothing came out. The Fresca was frozen solid.

I flung the can down and staggered over to Ed. "I need liquid," I croaked. "Coffee will do."

Ed pointed out that he was just building a fire, and that I'd have to be patient.

Even with clothes on I shivered uncontrollably. I was severely underdressed, mainly because I'd been living in Southern California too long, and my light jacket was no match for Sierra Nevada weather.

After a hot breakfast and coffee I was still freezing. I thought seriously of cutting arm and leg holes in my sleeping bag and wearing it, but Ed handed me one of his castoff rifles, and we trudged off into the woods. The hunting spot that Ed had in mind was a good mile and a half from the campsite. I had no idea how he found it because there wasn't any path to follow. Stumbling over dead branches in the predawn darkness, I was having strong second, third, and fourth thoughts about deer hunting.

At dawn we finally broke into a clearing. Ed turned to me and grinned. "This is it. You sit right here, an ideal spot. It's downwind. I'll be further down." He walked off into the trees.

I flopped down on a dead log, running my teeth over my fuzzy, coffee-royal tongue. An icy wind was blowing directly off the clearing, spearing right through my tissue-paper clothes, onto my blue, goose-bumped body.

For an hour I sat there, quivering, wondering why in the world I'd thought that deer hunting was fun when I was a teenager in the U.P. I gazed up, looking across the clearing.

A deer was standing on the far side. It had antlers.

I snapped the rifle to my shoulder. Weaver's old 30-06, I'm sure, was quite serviceable, but it lacked a scope. The buck was about 250 yards away, but squinting down the bare iron sights it looked like a thousand. My advanced stage of hypothermia didn't help. In my shaky grip, the rifle barrel jitterbugged around in a large ragged circle. Finally, I squeezed the trigger.

I squeezed it again, and again.

The safety was on.

Cursing, I flicked it off and fired. The deer looked up and trotted into the trees.

A minute later Ed came up. "Did you get it?" he asked.

"I didn't even give it a good scare," I said. "Let's go back to camp so I can crawl back into my sleeping bag."

That was the end of my deer hunting career. I want to wish you deer hunters the best of luck. One last piece of advice. Dress warm.

സൂരു

HAZARDOUS HOLIDAY TRAVEL

I'd guess many of you have horror stories about traveling during the holiday season. I have one, too.

In 1952 I was at the University of Michigan, pursuing an engineering degree; however, during the winter I had a student co-op job at White Sands Proving Ground, a government missile-testing facility in New Mexico. My sister, Esther—newly married—was living in Glendale, California, a suburb of Los Angeles. She invited me to travel from White Sands to spend Christmas with her and husband, Don.

California—the land of palm trees, Betty Grable, the Brown Derby, Rose Bowl, and Jack Benny! I'd seen California plenty of times in the movies but seriously doubted that I'd actually ever get there. Which brought up an interesting dilemma; how WAS I going to get there? I was church-mouse poor, and Esther hadn't volunteered to finance the trip.

Bob Kovacs, a fellow U of M co-oper at White Sands, reminded me that Douglas Aircraft had weekly flights from their plant in Santa Monica, California, to White Sands, delivering missiles for testing. On return flights the airplane was empty, and Kovacs reasoned that maybe Douglas would let me bum a ride out to California. It was such a fine idea that I invited Kovacs to come along.

Two weeks later Kovacs and I were at the White Sands Army Airport, suitcases in hand, staring dubiously at our so-called California transportation. The airplane we were about to board was an ancient C-47, a twin-engine, dumpy-looking craft with numerous aluminum patches on the fuselage and wings. It had been used during World War II to carry military cargo and paratroopers. The C-47 was affectionately labeled the "Gooney Bird," and it was easy to see why. It didn't look capable of getting off the ground.

The pilots arrived and told us to climb aboard. The only places to sit in the empty hull were the paratrooper jump seats along the sides of the fuselage. The pilots revved up the old crate and with a lot of rattling we took off. The big cargo compartment wasn't insulated, and with both piston engines at full throttle it was like the inside a giant bass drum. There wasn't any heat either. As we climbed toward cruising altitude, the inside temperature quickly dropped below freezing. Bob and I had heard that Southern California was sunny and warm, so all we were wearing were light clothes and windbreakers. But the cockpit was heated so I got up and stood behind the pilots to soak up warmth. However, when the plane began crossing over the Rockies we suddenly went into freefall in a severe air pocket. My body shot up, and I cracked my skull on the metal overhead and fell to the deck. The copilot jumped up, and dragged me back to the jump seats and buckled me in.

After five hours flying time—the C-47's cruising speed was only 175 miles per hour—we began to descend into the Los Angeles area. By now I had a golf-ball-size lump on the top of my noggin, a rotten headache, and the beginnings of a nasty head cold from the frigid airplane.

We landed at Clover Field in Santa Monica. Kovacs and I took our suitcases and left the airport property. In a second letter Esther had instructed us to meet her at a certain intersection in Glendale, claiming that she didn't drive long distances in Los Angeles traffic.

We had no map and no idea how far Glendale was from Santa Monica or how to catch a bus to get there.

We came upon a fellow backing his car out of a driveway and waved him down. He rolled his window down just a crack and eyed us suspiciously. I asked where we could catch a bus to Glendale. He stared at us like we were extraterrestrials. "A bus to Glendale? I haven't been on a bus in thirty years, and I certainly wouldn't know how to catch one to Glendale." He pointed off to the north. "Two blocks up. There's a bus that goes somewhere."

We caught a bus that went as far as West Los Angeles. Then another one to Beverly Hills. A third dropped us off in downtown Los Angeles where we were told to take one to Pasadena. That bus drove onto a truly scary road called the Pasadena Freeway. Four lanes of traffic all going in the same direction. No stop signs, traffic lights, or intersections. Crazed California drivers were all trying to outdo each other, barreling along at speeds over seventy miles an hour.

After three hours of bus rides we finally made connections with my sister. She took us to her apartment where I collapsed on the couch for the rest of the day.

For the next four days Don and Esther showed us all of the tourist sights—Hollywood & Vine, Sunset Boulevard, movie studios, and Grauman's Chinese Theatre. My nose ran through all four days.

Finally, the day arrived when Bob and I had to head back to White Sands. Since we had no plane ride back, we'd decided to hitchhike. Don and Esther were skeptical about that, but I assured them that we'd had plenty of experience hitchhiking in Michigan, so it wouldn't be a problem.

To give us a good head start, Don and Esther drove us to Indio, a desert town halfway to the Arizona border. It was a warm, sunny morning when we said our goodbyes, and Bob and I proceeded to hold out our thumbs.

Four hours later our thumbs were dusty and sunburned. California drivers never pick up hitchhikers because after all, anyone without a car in California must be mentally unstable or an escaped convict or both.

Our luck turned. A lady in a new Mercury stopped. We eagerly jumped in the back seat. Her name was Alice, and she was going to Blythe—eighty-five miles east—with her mother, a sweet, gray-haired little woman who was knitting an afghan in the passenger's seat.

Alice took off in a spray of gravel and in seconds cranked the Mercury up to ninety-five. Kovacs and I glanced at each other apprehensively but said nothing. Mother was humming a religious hymn as she knitted.

We drew up behind a car that was poking along at about ninety-two miles an hour. That was too slow for Alice so she pulled around to pass. But it wasn't easy overtaking this guy, and we were just creeping abreast when another car approached us, heading west. Did Alice brake and slip behind the car she was trying to pass? Absolutely not, California drivers aren't chickens. She forced that car onto the shoulder, and the approaching car hit the other shoulder as we shot down the centerline doing ninety-five. Horns blared. Alice's mother didn't drop a stitch.

Less than an hour later Alice dropped us off in Blythe where we kissed the ground. We hitchhiked unsuccessfully for another three hours and then used up the last of our cash for Greyhound Bus tickets to New Mexico.

I hope each and every one of you have a joyous holiday season. But if you can manage it, stay at home.

ဆၣ

WINTER GAMES

Nowadays they've got their video games and 70-inch TV sets, but I'm still amazed that I don't see more kids playing outside in the winter. When I was a kid, even too little to be able to zip up my own snowsuit, I practically LIVED outside during the winter months. My pals and I slid down every hilly street in Ishpeming, riding anything that slipped on ice and snow. A piece of cardboard worked just fine. If we had a large cardboard box, we got a running start at the top of the hill and jumped into the box. The boxes didn't last long, though, usually only one or two rides before being totally destroyed. Even faster was a piece of corrugated tin, although the sharp edges could open up a leg vein if you hit someone at the bottom of the hill.

For the ultimate in hair-raising speed, you slid down the hill on your old man's square-bladed snow shovel. You'd sit on the shovel blade, point the handle downhill, and push off. Beginner shovel riders mistakenly thought they could use the handle to steer. Not true. You were sitting on an unguided missile, but was it fast!

Finally one Christmas I got a Flexible Flyer sled, which was nice because I could steer it. I used to run the sled blades through wood-stove ashes to hone them for speed, but even then I don't think the sled was as fast as a good snow shovel.

In Ishpeming we were all ski jumpers. Every little location had its own ski jump built entirely by kids. Those who didn't have skis, jumped without them, using what were called gimmers—two barrel staves with homemade straps. Many times gimmers were harder to come by than real skis because the local moonshiners had a lock on the barrels.

If there was a really heavy winter storm, the fresh snow was too deep and fluffy for good sliding, so we jumped. Not ski jumping; we jumped off roofs of woodsheds and barns into snow drifts. It didn't make any difference what we jumped off, as long as it was high. The most fun was leaping off a barn roof into a very high drift and plunging into snow over our heads. We literally had to swim to the surface. Some carried the sport to the extreme by jumping into high drifts from strange roofs. You didn't know for sure if it was six feet of soft, pure snow or four inches of snow covering a six-foot pile of scrap iron. Needless to say, parents didn't think much of this sport.

And no winter would have been complete without some dumbbell taking the classic dare and sticking his tongue on cold metal. Sled blades were mostly used. The hapless dare taker would always panic when his tongue stuck to the blade. The trick was to stay calm and breathe heavily on the blade. The hot breath would release the tongue in seconds, but nobody seemed to think of that at the time.

Many successful construction careers began by building snow forts. Using shovels we painstakingly cut out large blocks of snow and built high fort walls. Why did we need a snow fort? To hold off enemy attacks, of course. By enemy I mean the Catholic kids. They had a fort of their own, and we regularly conducted raids on each other's forts, armed with snowballs. There was no love lost between the Catholic and Protestant kids, so an arms race resulted. We began putting chunks of iron ore in the core of the snowballs. Then we took it one step further and ran water on the surface of the snowball, creating a thick coating of ice. You definitely didn't want to be on the receiving end of one of those weapons of mass destruction. It would go clean through a snow-fort wall or, for that matter, take the siding off a house.

Even more physical was playing King of the Hill. One kid would be standing on top of a big snowbank, and the other kids would rush him, the object being to knock him off and claim the coveted spot for yourself. The name, King of the Hill, was a misnomer because the girls played too. In fact, it often became a battle of the sexes. If a particularly obnoxious girl was "King," you and your buddies would gleefully pluck her from her perch and chuck her head first into the snow. Great fun.

Another thing we did as kids—and I don't advise trying this—was shagging cars. Whenever we spotted someone getting into their car we'd sneak up behind it. The winter streets in Ishpeming were hard-packed slippery snow, and when the car started moving we'd hang onto to the rear bumper and get a ride. There's no thrill like sliding on your boots going thirty or forty miles an hour. You'd go as far as you wanted and then let go of the bumper. I should point out, though, that aside from the inherent danger of the sport there was an excellent chance of losing a mitten of two. When you tried to let go of the bumper your mitts were often frozen to it. Later on you'd have to go looking for the car to get your mitts back.

Just remember, shagging cars is dangerous, so don't try it. Besides, it would be embarrassing to try to explain to your wife or husband why you came home with only one glove.

The real problem these days is that adults are spoiling many of these winter pastimes. As soon as a decent layer of fresh snow falls, what happens? A big truck comes along and pours sand and salt all over the road. All of the good street hills are ruined for sliding. If I was a kid, I'd complain to somebody.

ഇⓇ

BRING BACK SIMPLE CARS

Getting into my Subaru the other morning to drive to Peggy Sue's for lunch, I spotted a note on the windshield. A guy apologized for dinging my car as he was pulling a trailer out of my apartment-house parking lot. The honest soul left his name and phone number. (Only in the U.P. does this happen.)

The Subaru had a broken plastic tail-light cover, a tiny crease on the rear panel, and a few minor scratches and a pinhead-size hole in the rear bumper. I wouldn't have even noticed the damage.

Over at Peggy Sue's I asked my friend Jeff what he thought it would cost to get it fixed.

He looked at the Subaru. "Oh, about seven or eight hundred dollars."

Good old Jeff, always joking. "C'mon," I said, "eight hundred dollars? It's just a little ding and a broken piece of plastic! I say three hundred, tops! You're hundreds of dollars off!"

My insurance agent instructed me to take the car to their preferred body-repair shop for an estimate. Jeff WAS hundreds of dollars off. The estimate I got was $1246.

$1246. That's more than I paid for my first five cars combined.

I looked at the breakdown of the estimate. It seems that they can't just replace the red plastic tail-light cover, they have to install the whole tail light assembly unit, costing $136. That's the only way they can get it from the manufacturer. And what I thought was the bumper is really a cover for the bumper. These days automakers feel that steel bumpers have no visual appeal to prospective buyers, so they put a sexy-looking cover over the bumper, made out of plastic or something. If there's a hole in it, the cover can't be fixed so the body-shop people throw it away and install a new one. Remember back in the old days if a friend of yours got stuck in the snow, you'd push his car with yours to get it loose? Don't even think about doing that anymore. You'd mash up that bumper cover good, and trust me, those things cost a few bucks.

Also on the estimate was an item labeled "Paint and associated materials—$206." This was to touch up the little crease in the rear panel. I once painted a whole house for less money than that. The problem is that cars now come in a zillion different colors, so a specially programmed computer tells you how to mix the paint.

But according to what I heard at the body shop, the job on my Subaru is small potatoes. Suppose you're driving a three-year-old Chevy and get into a fender bender that happens to activate the air bags. You may walk away from the car without a scratch, but the Chevy is totaled. You see, the air bags are expendable, and the cost to replace them runs over four thousand dollars.

Is all of this modern technology that's gone into automobiles a good thing? A few years ago I had an Oldsmobile which ran fine until it suddenly began sputtering going up hills. I took it to a mechanic who hooked the Olds up to his engine analyzer and then told me that the air to fuel ratio was going out of whack on hills.

I nodded knowledgeably. "So you adjust the carburetor, right?"

"Cars don't have carburetors anymore."

"Oh."

"It's the car's central computer. It monitors and adjusts the air to fuel ratio as you drive, but as the car gets older this computer can begin making unreliable decisions."

"You mean my Oldsmobile has developed Alzheimer's?"

"Well, yeah, something like that."

It cost me over $400 to improve the Oldsmobile's memory.

How many of you have the nerve to look under the hood of your car these days? I don't do that anymore. It depresses me because I don't know what any of that stuff is. It's a rat's nest of alien electrogadgets lashed together with miles of strange wires and tubes. I imagine that nowadays there's a lot of conversations between car owners and mechanics that go something like this:

<u>car owner</u> So, what's wrong with my car?

<u>mechanic</u> Nothing much. You just need a new grommet whacker.

<u>car owner</u> Are they expensive?

<u>mechanic</u> Not at all. A grommet whacker only costs a buck and a half.

<u>car owner</u> Fine. Put one in.

<u>mechanic</u> Of course, there's labor. You see, in order to get at the grommet whacker I gotta pull out the magnetogrinder, the sonic camshaft analyzer, the robotic exhaust conditioner, and, oh yeah, the engine. The labor ought'a run, oh, about six thousand dollars.

If we could bring back simple cars, they'd cost a heck of a lot less money to fix. Put carburetors back in them like the one I had in my Model A. It had three moving parts and worked just fine. Air bags are good things, but why can't they be used again? Just suck out the air with a vacuum cleaner and refold them. And another thing, there are enough computers in this world, we don't need them driving the car for us. I never minded cranking the windows up and down by hand. In fact, it improved the muscle tone in my arms. Finally, I want to have a car with a good sturdy bumper without a wimpy cover so I can actually bump something if I want to.

ഇരുജ

THE THRILL OF WALLPAPERING

Ever since I moved into my apartment six years ago I've been quite satisfied with it. It's in a quiet neighborhood in east Marquette, surrounded by historic nineteenth century mansions. The living room is huge with a view of Lake Superior. A really nice place. But nothing is perfect, and one thing in the apartment has always bugged me. The bedroom wallpaper.

The wallpaper pattern is teeming with writhing little Batmobile-blue leaves and vines that appear ready to leap right off the paper and wind themselves around my neck. I can hear those vines creeping into my bed at night. This paper has offended me for six years so I'm finally changing it.

I don't mean that I'll do the wallpapering MYSELF. Uh-uh. I know my limitations. There's only a few things that I'm handy at, and wallpapering isn't one of them. People keep telling me how simple it is, but I know better.

When I was seven years old my mother decided that spring that she wanted new wallpaper in our living room, or front room as we called it back then. She was about to hire a professional paperhanger when my father butted in.

"Why spend all that money," he said. "Wallpapering is easy. We kin do it ourselves and save a bundle."

A few days later all of the front-room furniture had been pushed into the kitchen or out in the yard. A couple of saw horses with planks across them took center stage in the bare room. My parents were ready to start wallpapering, although my mother wasn't too enthusiastic about it.

The first order of business was to put up the ceiling paper. Back in those days people also papered their ceilings. How many of you have papered a ceiling? Lots of fun, eh?

To save even more money the old man had decided to make his own paste, mixing flour and water. When he began spreading it on the back of the ceiling paper my mother told him that the paste was too lumpy. He said it'd be just fine after he smoothed out the paper on the ceiling.

An hour later the few lonely strips of new paper sticking to the ceiling looked as though several large chipmunks had gotten trapped underneath. My mother was loudly announcing that the paste was still too lumpy. The old man, his hair now liberally decorated with white pasty lumps, was defending his handiwork using very salty language. My mother quickly shooed me outside.

Just as quickly I snuck back into the house in order not to miss any of the action. I peeked in from the kitchen just as the old man was struggling to stick another pasted strip to the ceiling. He just about had it fastened in place when the paper broke loose, landing with a splat on top of his head. The paper was so soggy that it split apart and settled onto his shoulders.

Right then Mummu Harju, my paternal grandmother and family matriarch, walked in and saw the whole thing. I never found out exactly what she told my father because she was yelling in Finn, but he quickly tore the ceiling paper off his body and scrambled to the floor. The next day the professional paperhanger came in and finished the job.

The only time I had first-hand experience with wallpapering was in 1964. Joanne, my second wife-to-be, and I were lying on the couch in my modest rented house in Santa Monica, California, involved in some steamy necking (not what you think, this was 1964.)

She looked up over my shoulder. "Do you know there's a big chunk of loose plaster on your ceiling ready to fall down?"

"So what?" I muttered hotly in her ear.

"It's going to come down and hurt somebody."

The next thing I knew we were over at a builder supply store buying plaster and various associated tools to apply the plaster. Later, when the job was done, she remarked, "Now there's a big white spot up there. We've got to paint the whole ceiling."

You have to understand that I was totally infatuated with this woman, so I went along with whatever she suggested. Back to the builder-supply store for paint, rollers, and brushes.

"The ceiling looks great," she said, "but it sure makes the walls look tacky. Let's put up new wallpaper."

"I don't know a thing about wallpapering," I said.

"It's easy, especially with two of us doing it."

Because the old wallpaper was in such bad shape, Joanne decided that we had to steam it off. We rented a steamer and fired it up. What she hadn't mentioned was that a wallpaper steamer takes off EVERYTHING. Layer upon layer of ancient wallpaper and paint dating back to the Spanish American War fell off the walls. With it came several large hunks of plaster. Back to the store for more plaster.

This had now turned into a major effort. Since we both had jobs we were doing this work in the evenings. Prepping the walls was hot dusty work, and we took to refreshing ourselves with a curious cocktail consisting of apple juice and vodka which didn't enhance my renovating skills one bit.

Apparently wallpapering is in the genes because I was about as good at it as my old man. When we began putting up the paper

I was so inept that Joanne finally demoted me to mixing the drinks and other lowly gofer duties.

A year or so later we were married and had just purchased a house in Hermosa Beach. The day we were moving in Joanne looked at the living-room walls and said, "That wallpaper is terrible. It's got to go."

I ran screaming into the street.

We finally compromised. She did the wallpapering and I drove back and forth to the builder-supply store.

So you can see why I'm subcontracting out the bedroom wallpaper job. Except I've still got to pick out a pattern. I've become obsessively fussy in my senior years because for two weeks I've been lugging sample books back and forth from the Marquette Wallpaper and Paint Company and haven't selected a pattern yet. They've got over two hundred sample books and each book has about one hundred patterns. That's twenty thousand to chose from. I need help. I wish Martha Stewart lived around here.

☙❧

HAIR-RAISING TALES

A few weeks ago I was having my hair cut at Design Lines Too, an upscale hair salon in Harvey. Michelle, an attractive young stylist, was making pleasant conversation as she contoured my dwindling supply of hair. The whole experience was very enjoyable, and it got me thinking that this was definitely not my father's haircut.

I mean that literally. My father gave me my first haircuts. The old man saw no reason to foolishly spend money bringing me to a barber when he could do the job himself. With a bath towel around my neck to catch the loose hair, he'd unceremoniously perch me on the edge of the kitchen table and start in.

The towel also caught blood and tears. My father used a pair of those old spring-action hand clippers which, if the blades weren't really sharp—and they never were—pulled the hair out by the roots. I'd yell and cry, but the old man would just tighten his vice-like grip on my head and clip away, growling, "Shaddup so I kin get this done!"

My father eventually broke down and took me for my first visit to a real barber. That experience was scarier than the old man's brutal haircuts. I was sitting on a board laid across the arms of the barber's chair when the barber fired up his electric clippers with an ominous whine. I almost wet my pants. I thought that the old man had conned me into a dentist's chair, and I was going to get a tooth pulled.

In high school I needed all the hair I could grow in order to shape it into the latest guy pompadour style of 1950. First, I'd carefully blend in a half pound of Wildroot Creme Oil until my hair was thickened to the consistency of bread dough. Using a comb I'd expertly sculpt a towering wave that leaned over my forehead like the surf at Hawaii's Banzai Pipeline. It was high enough to pick up radio signals, and if I stopped suddenly, the whole thing was in danger of collapsing over my eyes.

At the University of Michigan men's hair styles were totally different. Instead of the soaring mass of glop I'd been sporting in high school I had to get a flattop. A flattop haircut was just exactly that, flat on top. In fact, a proper flattop was pool-table flat, and it took a barber with rock-steady hands to get it just right. Being an eager beaver engineering student, I had to check the flatness after every haircut. In my dorm room I'd run a large drafting T square across the top of my head to check for any unwanted high or low spots.

During the 1960's I was living in California and regressed back to my pre-high-school hair style which was no hair style at all. I have typical Finn hair, very fine and soft, and unless it's pasted down with large quantities of gel or cut very short any little breeze will swirl it around like a haystack in a tornado. But that was okay because this was during my beatnik period. I had grown a scroungy beard, drank cheap wine out of large jugs, played folk guitar in smokey coffee houses, and on weekends dressed like I'd shopped for clothes in a dumpster. My Pick-Up-Sticks hair fit the image perfectly.

But then one night in the early seventies I was at my girlfriend's house when a friend of ours, Russ Kolemainen, came over. Russ was a Finn and had hair like mine, all over the place. Except that night he looked entirely different. Russ had gotten his hair permed, and the curls made him positively handsome. He had been going out with a beautician who moonlighted in her apartment in the evenings. I got her name and telephone number and made an appointment right away.

For years I'd been living in Southern California. Guys out there think nothing of getting face lifts, tummy tucks, or wearing gold rings on parts of their body where no one should wear gold rings. However, I couldn't escape my U.P. upbringing where real men would have chosen death by firing squad over getting their hair permed. So on the night of my first perm I was in a terrible state of anxiety. But my friend Russ really looked good with his curly hair, so I grabbed a gallon jug of wine and took off.

The beautician eyed the wine when I walked in her door. "Is that a gift for me?"

"No, it's liquid courage for me. Have you got a large glass?"

She sat me down on a kitchen chair and began putting curlers in my hair. I was facing a large mirror because for some perverse reason beauticians believe their customers want to watch everything that's going on. The last thing in the world I wanted to see was my hair up in curlers. I drank the wine faster.

Three hours later we were done, and I felt very good about the whole experience. Of course, one reason might have been the half gallon of wine I'd drunk during the process. She could have done me up in pink pigtails, and I would have thought it was just grand. My girlfriend had to come over and drive me home.

I kept my curly hair until I moved back up here in 1996. I let it grow out because I couldn't stand to see my old high-school classmates doubling over with laughter whenever they saw me. I don't worry about my hair anymore. It doesn't flop around much because there's a lot less of it now. Besides, up here you wear a cap ten months out of the year.

෨෬

SPRING HAS SPRUNG

The other day I noticed the first sign of spring. No, it wasn't a robin pulling a half-frozen worm out of the ground. I drove my freshly washed Buick to Ishpeming, and when I got back home the car was still clean. After six months of plowing through slush and sand and salt on the roads, this is a real sign of spring.

When I was a kid the most exciting rite of spring was taking off my long underwear. All winter long I wore that heavy, itchy second skin twenty-four hours a day, and it was cause for celebration when I could finally peel it off. Without the long johns I was suddenly lighter and quicker. I felt sure I could jump off the woodshed roof and fly through the air like Superman. Girls enjoyed an added bonus. Without long underwear beneath their stockings they no longer had that "piano leg" look.

Every spring my mother would go absolutely nuts. It seems that our little family had been living in a foul pig pen all winter long, and she was going to singlehandedly clean it up. Every square inch of every surface in the house was thoroughly scrubbed, even the ceilings. The lace curtains were taken down from the windows, washed and carefully put on stretchers to dry. She dragged all the rugs out of the house, threw them over the clothesline, and knocked the bejezzus out of them with a carpet beater.

My father had his work, too. The storm windows had to be taken down and the screens put up. There must have been some sneaky little winter varmint in our woodshed that liked to nibble on metal because every spring there were always several holes in the screens that the old man had to patch before he put them up. Invariably there was always one screen missing. It usually wasn't found until early fall. The old man would also take our kitchen wood stove apart and scrub out the insides with a stiff brush. I don't think that job was his idea, though.

When the weather warmed sufficiently, my friend Jeff and I would embark on a furtive spring construction project. Behind our houses in south Ishpeming was a steep hill. Tons of snow melting on this hill would create a swift runoff. Halfway up the hill Jeff and I would build a dam of snow that collected a spectacular amount of this melt-off in a short time. At the proper moment, like when some matronly neighbor was walking on the road below, we'd "blow" the dam, sending a monumental cascade of icy water toward our hapless target. Great fun.

When the ground got dry enough it was time to play marbles. We didn't play the standard game where you try to knock marbles out of a circle. We played what I called "pot marbles"—some called it "holesy"—where you dug a hole or "pot" in the dirt. From a line ten feet away everyone took a turn pitching his marble at the pot. The closest player got first crack at shooting marbles into the pot. The thrill of the game was that you got to keep all the marbles you shot into the pot. This was called "keepsies." I never told my mother about "keepsies" because gambling—even for cheap marbles—was unchristian.

And of course we started playing baseball. This meant winding fresh electrician's tape around the loose seams in the baseball and more tape around the cracks in our bats so they'd last another season.

You don't see anyone flying kites anymore, but when I was a kid we all flew kites in the spring, or in my case tried to fly a kite. You could buy a kite kit at Newberry's for a dime, but I usually made my own because the life span of my kites was very short. They would meet sad, untimely ends, hopelessly tangled in power lines or tall trees, or from sudden power dives into the ground. When it came to kite flying I was the Charley Brown of Ishpeming. I never could get them off the ground. I tried different designs—lighter paper, a longer tail—but nothing worked. Later on I took two courses in aerodynamics at the U of M but never solved the mystery of flying a kite.

Most important of all, springtime started a countdown of the remaining days left in the school year. Even the most arithmetic-challenged lame-brain kid could tell you to the hour how much time was left until school was out. Spring was nice but summer was even better.

I hope you're all getting out and enjoying our wonderful spring weather. Of course, Mother Nature has a real quirky sense of humor when it comes to U.P. weather. On the day that this piece hits the street we might be having a late April blizzard. In that case put the column away and read it again in June.

෩෨

A FISH STORY

Over the years people have asked why I don't write columns about fishing. The reason is simple; I'm a rotten fisherman. I've spent countless hours fruitlessly drowning worms, and who wants to read that? I do have one fish story—a true one, what else?—which is appropriate for this time of year.

In 1950 I was a junior at Republic High School. During noon hour a bunch of us would hang around the Standard gas station, drinking Coke and swapping lies about our conquests with girls. But one Friday noon in April one of the guys changed the subject and said, "Hey, the suckers are running. Let's go get some tomorrow."

In the spring these bottom-feeding fish would spawn in the streams. I'd never fished for suckers, being a brook trout angler myself, and even the brook trout were pretty safe when I dropped my line in the water.

"What do you use for bait when you fish for suckers?" I asked.

The gang sneered at my stupid question. "You don't need bait when suckers are running," someone said. "They're so thick you can spear 'em or net 'em."

Everyone got enthusiastic about the idea. The guys realized I didn't know much about fishing, but they all wanted me to come along. It could have been because I was the only one who had a car. The next day six of us piled into my Model A Ford and headed for a stream out along the Michigamme River road.

The idea of getting fish by launching projectiles at them appealed to me so I'd borrowed a three-prong fishing spear from my Uncle Arvid, and as a backup I'd also brought an old bow with some arrows. The rest of the gang took along a variety of weapons, nets, and potato sacks for our catch.

One guy directed us to a stream where he'd had luck catching spawning suckers in years past so I parked the Model A, and we edged up to the water.

Sure enough, you could see plenty of big fat suckers in the shallow water. I took aim at one of them and let fly with the spear.

Right then I received my first lesson in applied physics, specifically optical diffraction. I found out that when you spot a fish in the water it really isn't where you see it because the light waves bend when they enter the water. After several unsuccessful attempts the prongs on the spear were badly blunted from hitting nothing but rocks. I picked up my bow and arrows but had no better luck.

Then one of the guys had a brilliant idea. He instructed us to wade into the water. He went fifty yards upstream, jumped in and began beating the water with his fists as he walked toward us.

Within seconds the stream was boiling with fish as the panicked suckers swam toward us. The water was numbingly cold on my legs, but I forgot about it when I began feeling the fish thumping into me. I reached down, grabbed one with my bare hands and flung it on the stream bank. For a few seconds I watched the fish flopping in the grass. I hadn't had much exposure to suckers, and I'd forgotten how ugly they are.

For the next hour we frantically scooped up suckers and threw them on shore. We took turns beating the water and catching fish. This was my kind of fishing—lots of action.

Thoroughly satisfied with our fishing expedition, we happily loaded all of the suckers into sacks and headed back to Republic. I dropped the gang off and drove home.

After parking in the yard I noticed that there were still many potato sacks full of suckers on the back floor of the Model A. I had caught quite a few fish myself but not nearly as many as were still in the car. Apparently some of my friends had forgotten to take their fish with them.

I grabbed a couple of the heavy sacks and lugged them into the kitchen.

"What's that?" my mother asked.

"Fish," I announced proudly.

She looked in one of the sacks. "These are suckers."

"Yeah, why don't you cook some up for supper?"

"Have you ever eaten suckers?"

"No."

"Well, you won't eat any in this house. Get them out of here."

Crestfallen, I took the suckers back out to the car. I drove to some of the neighbor's houses and graciously offered them all the fish they wanted. Everyone looked at me kind of funny, chuckled, and closed their doors.

I was getting the definite impression that suckers weren't high on anyone's list for fine dining. Making matters worse, the Model A was taking on a pungent aura that was definitely going to cramp my style picking up girls that night.

In final desperation, with the car windows wide open, I sped over to my grandparent's house on the other end of town. My grandmother looked in the sack, gave me a sad smile, and shook her head. But my grandfather, an ex-lumberjack known to eat almost anything, looked at the ugly fish and grinned widely.

"Suckers! I like boiled suckers!"

What followed was a heated discussion in Finn between my

grandparents. My grandmother paced the floor, violently shook her head and muttered ominously. Grandfather nodded his head vigorously, waved his arms around, and chattered away. Finally, he took the sack of suckers and led me outside. "Leave 'em in the woodshed." he said. "I take care of 'em."

That was the last I saw of the suckers. It was my most successful fishing expedition by far, but no one was impressed. I never found out how many of them my grandfather ate, but I remember noticing that he had a very healthy-looking vegetable garden that summer. I suspect that the final resting place of most of the great sucker catch was beneath the carrots.

೫೦೮೩

LIFE IN THE BIG CITY

As many of you know, I was born in the U.P. but spent many years in Southern California, purchased two houses there, married two women, divorced two women, and attempted to pay for all that by working in the aerospace business. After taking early retirement I moved back here in 1996 and became a struggling, starving writer. I just returned from a visit to the kingdom of Arnold Schwarzenegger, and here's what's currently happening out there.

One in eight Americans live in California; that's thirty-seven million people, and they're all driving on the freeway. As my flight came in for a landing at LAX, we passed over the 405 Freeway. At midday the traffic was bumper to bumper. In Los Angeles, rush-hour traffic is a thing of the past; it's 24/7 gridlock now.

Nevertheless, I ignored the grim possibility of becoming permanently entombed in a stream of stalled Chevys and Fords and rented a car from AVIS.

L.A. drivers have a more serious problem than traffic. The *Los Angeles Times* was running front-page accounts of the Freeway Shooter. It seems that someone has been pulling alongside of unsuspecting freeway motorists and opening fire. The latest one occurred the day I arrived. Since the middle of March several freeway shootings have occurred, resulting in four deaths and wounding of others. Police are struggling for clues but so far have made no arrests. A California Highway Patrol high-ranking official made a statement reflecting the true flavor of life in the big city. "We don't want the public to think there's an onslaught of shootings. We are actually on pace to have fewer shootings this year, and remember, these shootings are taking place in three counties that are heavily traveled with high populations."

That means, don't be disturbed, this is pretty much business as usual.

Speaking of freeways, Los Angeles has its own reality show which could be called "Catch Me If You Can." The California Highway Patrol will attempt to pull some bozo over for a traffic violation when the guy puts the pedal to the metal and takes off. The cops don't even try to run him down but merely follow the offender, waiting for him to make a mistake or run out of gas. Of course, experienced scofflaws out there always have a full tank of gas in anticipation of a run-in with the police, so these freeway pursuits can last for hours and cover hundreds of miles.

In no time newscopters are swarming overhead, and every scheduled TV program is bumped in order to cover the chase. It's great fun to watch because there's no commercials. Naturally, most sponsors hate freeway chases except, perhaps, the maker of the car that the chasee is driving.

While I was out there I took my usual early morning walk. The only other pedestrians were walking their dogs, and they all gave me suspicious glances because I didn't have a dog. No one out there walks merely for the sake of walking. They figured that I must have been a second-story man heading home after a heavy night of burglaring.

During my walk I always stopped at Ralph's Market in Marina del Rey to pick up a morning copy of the *Los Angeles Times*. I like to look at the classifieds to see how much it would cost me to live out there now. On the west side of L.A. where I used to live I saw practically no homes for sale under a half-million dollars. Many rather ordinary-looking houses run over a million because of the location. There was one exception; the ad said, "Cute starter home - $300,000." This is for young couples who can't afford anything better. The average rent for an apartment like I used to have is about $2200 a month now. As if I didn't have enough incentive to stay in the U.P.

I know I shouldn't pick on California so much, but let's face it, there's so much to pick on—the high crime rate, high cost of living, waiting in long lines for everything, and waiting for that big 8.0 earthquake which is supposed to happen one of these days. Actually, it was a very good trip. I had a great time visiting old friends, including my long-time sweetie, Pat. The weather was perfect—sunny and seventy. But when I got off the plane at Sawyer, with the temperature much chillier than California, I said to myself, boy, it's really good to be back home.

అంశ

WILDERNESS WOMAN

The U.P. has a long history of being home to eccentric recluses living deep in the woods. When I was in high school in Republic my parents ran a small restaurant. Once a month these guys—most of them pulp cutters—would steal into town for groceries, chewing tobacco, stiff drinks at the local bars, and a good hot meal at our café. The following day they faded back into the bush, having had their fill of the civilized life for another month.

These loners are mostly gone now. There are still folks living in the woods up here, but today most of them have comfortable ties with the outside world—all utilities piped in for TV sets, Internet service, microwave ovens, hot showers and flush toilets. Modern technology has a sneaky way of compromising solitude.

But recently I've become good friends with someone who remains a staunch holdout against creeping civilization. This person is a petite five foot four with long hair. That's right, a woman.

Marie—a pseudonym to protect her privacy—owns a log cabin on a hundred-plus acres, enough land so there'll never be close neighbors. She lives alone. Well, not quite; there's a very large Alaskan malamute guard dog, four cats, and a zillion birds that eat at the feeders. Then there are deer, foxes, coyotes, chipmunks, porcupines, flying squirrels, pine martins, and even the occasional bear, wolf, and moose. Marie has plenty of company; just not the human variety.

Why is this woman living out there? For one thing, she likes critters more than people. In fact, she doesn't even eat anything that walks or flies. Not only is Marie an animal lover, she's an animal expert. She has an Master of Science degree in Wildlife Management, and—get this—a major in Black Bear Habitat Management. For years she worked for the U.S. Forest Service in Minnesota, doing close-up research on lifestyle patterns of black bears. I mean, REALLY close-up research. On one occasion a bear cub climbed into her lap while mama bear warily looked on. (Don't try this at home).

Marie's place is ideal for studying wildlife. It's several miles down a rough dirt road requiring four-wheel drive much of the year. There are no utility lines in this neck of the woods. Marie uses solar panels and a wind turbine to charge a bank of batteries for electricity, so she has to be thrifty with energy usage. "I vacuum the rugs only when the sun shines," Marie claims.

There's one faucet in the house, fed by gravity. A fresh-water spring at the top of the hill behind the cabin flows downhill into a large stainless-steel tank above the kitchen faucet. A primitive system, but it's the best water I've ever tasted.

Marie has an outhouse, but not the usual model. This one has a wide glassed-in picture window so you can sit inside and gaze out at the natural surroundings. No need for modesty, there's no one else out there but the animals.

How many of you women have the knack for whipping up hot meals on a wood stove? Marie does it regularly on an ancient cast-iron monster that her great-grandmother used. Another wood stove on the bottom level heats the whole cabin through iron floor registers like we used to have when I was a kid.

Just supplying the stoves with wood is a job. Every summer Marie harvests timber from her property to get ten cords of firewood needed for heat and cooking. She cuts the timber and hauls the logs to her shed for splitting and stacking. Last year she finally went hi-tech with a gasoline-driven wood splitter, but before that she split all ten cords by hand, using an eight-pound splitting maul. One day she gave me a live demonstration, expertly splitting several hefty logs with the maul. I tried it myself and almost lost a foot.

Winters out there are especially tough. Marie's driveway is a steep, winding, two-rut trail climbing a third of a mile up to her cabin. In the dead of winter it has to be cleared of snow three or four times a week. In that terrain a vehicle with a front-end plow can't get in there to do the job, so Marie pushes a snow blower up and down the driveway. She says she really enjoys it, but I don't know, I did it once, and it's a lot like work.

The ashes from the wood stoves now come in handy because even with a clean driveway her four-wheel-drive vehicle needs more traction.

It's a hard way to live with many sacrifices, but there is an upside. Marie hasn't had a cold in over a decade, has never had the flu, she's agile and strong and looks at least twenty years younger than her true age. It's obvious that her lifestyle is healthy. Of course, it also helps that she gave up rubbing elbows with bears.

ഐരു

THE FIRST PROM

Recently I've noticed high-schoolers on the streets of Marquette in fancy gowns and tuxedos on their way to spring proms. A look of apprehension on some of the faces, and I can understand why. It's their first prom. A first prom is a critical rite of passage and never taken lightly. I know. At one time I faced that ordeal.

In 1949 I was a sophomore at Republic High School. In order to avoid becoming a complete social misfit, sophomores had to attend the spring Junior Prom.

One major obstacle was that I didn't have a car. For weeks I agonized over this dilemma until one day I somehow talked my uncle Arne into letting me borrow his '36 Chevrolet for the event. Arne didn't realize that the ink on my driver's license was barely dry at the time.

By now the prom was only days away, and I had to address my second priority: finding a date. I frantically asked several girls, but they already had dates. Or so they said. Finally, by some miracle, I found a girl who agreed to go with me. I won't disclose her name because she must have been truly desperate at the time, and I'm sure she wouldn't want to be connected with this story.

The first thing I had to do was clean and wax the car. Applying wax to Arne's ramshackle Chevy was like putting lipstick on a pig, but nevertheless I attacked the job with gusto. I checked the fan belt and the air in the spare tire, and as a further precautionary measure put a five-gallon can of water in the trunk in case of radiator boilover.

On the big day I awoke with a tight knot in my stomach. My total experience with the opposite sex had been limited to furtive smooching in the back of a dark bus coming back from high-school basketball games. I'd never been on a real date, and I didn't know what to expect.

I went to a neighbor's sauna and sweated adolescent poisons from my system. Back home I inserted a new blade in my Gillette safety razor which really wasn't safe at all because along with the four whiskers on my chin I also managed to lop off a fresh crop of pimples. A thick coat of Clearasil stanched the flow of blood and covered up the acne.

For the formal occasion I put on brand-new underwear and punched my arms through the sleeves of a heavily starched white shirt. Next came the suit. My mother had ordered it from the Montgomery Ward catalog. She'd reasoned that I'd gain seventy-five pounds by the time I graduated from high school, so the suit would have fit a buffalo. My fingertips barely peeked out of the mammoth sleeves. The shoulder pads would have done any NFL lineman proud, and the lapels were as big as ironing boards. Lastly, I tackled my hair. I blended in several ounces of Wildroot Creme Oil, kneading the hair into a thick, doughy texture. With a comb I sculpted a towering pompadour that leaned over my forehead like a tidal wave. I jumped in the Chevy and took off.

I barely recognized my date. She was decked out in a chiffon ankle-length gown, had freshly curled hair, makeup, and half-inch-long eyelashes. Women who looked like that were only in the movies. I was afraid to get close to her.

On the way to the high-school gymnasium I attempted to impress her with my driving skill by double-clutching through the gears. Actually, that was the only way I knew how to shift. My Uncle Arvid had taught me to drive in his huge war-surplus command vehicle where double-clutching was necessary.

The gymnasium had been decorated by the junior class for the gala occasion. Dozens of card tables and metal folding chairs along the walls were festooned with orange and black crepe-paper streamers—our school colors. The modest budget of the junior class couldn't support live entertainment, so a Wurlitzer jukebox procured from a local bar was cranking out the current hot tunes—"Buttons and Bows," "Once in Love with Amy," "Riders in the Sky," and "Golden Earrings."

We sat down at a card table, clutching paper cups filled with a mystery punch. Now came a critical juncture in the evening. Dancing. In the solitude of my bedroom I had stumbled through the intricate mechanics of the box step, but I'd never performed in public and never with a partner. I listened carefully to the tempo of the music and rightly concluded that my box step wasn't going to hack it with a song like "Zip-A-Dee-Doo-Dah."

"The Blue Skirt Waltz" began playing, and my date looked at me hopefully. It sounded slow enough, and I thought, what the heck, here goes. We ventured onto the basketball floor and lurched into "The Blue Skirt Waltz."

It was a shaky start. Every fourth beat or so I tromped on my partner's foot. It got better when I began counting one-two-three, one-two-three, matching my steps to the music as I maneuvered through the box step. When my date gave me an odd look I realized that I'd been counting aloud.

Somebody got the message that the boys couldn't dance the fast numbers because soon the Wurlitzer was only playing slow, dreamy waltzes. My partner and I dutifully box-stepped into the evening.

The horde of sweating bodies on the dance floor sent the

gymnasium temperature soaring. Soon my shoes felt like they were riveted to my feet. My once-crisp shirt was limp with perspiration, but the collar remained stiff, gnawing into my skin like a saw blade.

My date was faring no better. Her curly hair was unwinding like a tired clock spring. Freckles emerged through the rapidly melting layer of makeup on her flushed cheeks. One eye had lashes an inch longer than the other. She had developed a serious limp from being stepped on repeatedly.

Finally, after what seemed like three lifetimes, the Wurlitzer went dark. The prom was over. Earlier in the evening I'd entertained the idea that after the dance I'd take my date out for a bite to eat. But my stomach was still pitching and rolling dangerously from the pressures of the day, and I didn't want to end the evening tossing my cookies in front of my date. I drove her home, and she seemed quite content with that. We'd both had enough.

৪৩

A DOGHOUSE TALE

I always watch the morning network shows—NBC's Today and ABC's Good Morning America—because many off-the-wall happenings in the world are grist for my columns. One I saw the other day is a prime example.

A specialty carpenter was a guest on the Today show, impressing Matt Lauer with his latest creations: upscale doghouses. These weren't your run-of-the-mill doghouses. They were more like small (but not all that small) versions of Scarlett O'Hare's plantation home in "Gone With The Wind." Some featured paned windows complete with louvered shutters. One had an authentic-looking brick chimney which I don't imagine was functional, but then again who knows? Another doghouse was a French chateau with a copper roof, bay window, and a hardwood floor. You could order a custom-built miniature replica of your own house complete with landscaping, air-conditioning, and hand-painted wallpaper.

Matt Lauer asked the carpenter about the price tag on these pooch palaces.

"A few of them are going on Ebay," the carpenter replied. "They might fetch about ten-thousand apiece."

Ten-thousand dollars for a doghouse. That's about five times what my old man paid for the Ishpeming house I was born in.

This TV piece jogged my memory of an unusual doghouse I once owned or rather I should say a doghouse that owned ME.

In 1965 my second wife, Joanne, and I bought a house in Hermosa Beach, California. We'd no sooner moved in when Joanne decided that since we were homeowners now it would be nice if we got a dog. A friend of mine had a litter of German Shepherd puppies. He cagily plied us with beer one Sunday afternoon while we looked over the puppies, and I wound up buying two of them.

Our new home had a backyard that ran the length of the house. After I put up a tall fence and bricked in the yard, we had a perfect dog run.

"Now we need a doghouse back there," Joanne said.

I agreed, and told her that I'd make one as soon as I attended to a jillion other things that our new house needed.

But my wife took matters into her own hands. Her sister Paula and her husband, Bill, were housing contractors in Roland Heights, a suburb of Los Angeles. The phone conversation went something like this.

<u>Joanne</u> "Paula, do your carpenters ever have any spare time on the job?"

<u>Paula</u> "Sure, what do you need?"

<u>Joanne</u> "A doghouse for our new puppies."

<u>Paula</u> "No problem. How big a doghouse do you want?"

<u>Joanne</u> "Oh, I don't know. Those Shepherds are going to get to be pretty large dogs. Why don't we say, oh, about six feet by six feet by six feet."

<u>Paula</u> "You got it."

A week later the doghouse was ready. Joanne took our pickup truck to Roland Heights to get it while I was at work.

I had to work late, and by the time I got home it was dark. Joanne took me out to the backyard and told me to look over the fence. A towering, dark shape loomed in the sand next to the alleyway, blotting out the evening stars.

"What's that?" I asked.

"The doghouse," Joanne replied.

"THAT'S our doghouse?"

"Actually, it's only half the doghouse. I had to make two trips. A couple of the carpenters came back with me to help unload the first piece, but the doghouse roof is still on the pickup. We'll need some help to get it off the truck."

The next morning I took a good look at our "doghouse." It was massive. The frame was made from 2X4's and 2X8's, and the walls and roof were 3/4" plywood. The whole thing easily weighed half a ton.

That Saturday, with the promised reward of a large keg of beer, I conned seven or eight of my friends from work to come over and help put the doghouse in the backyard. With much straining, grunting, and cursing we managed to hoist the two sections over the fence and put them together in the backyard.

Fully assembled, it looked like Snoopie's doghouse except that it was big enough to house Paul Bunyon's ox. I could stand upright inside, and I'm not short.

Joanne let the dogs out of the kitchen into the backyard to inspect their new home. The two puppies took one look at the gigantic structure and ran back into the kitchen. They were afraid of the doghouse.

Joanne said to me, "They'll probably like it a lot better when you paint it and put shingles on the roof."

Which was my job the following weekend. After two gallons of paint and three boxes of shingles, the doghouse looked more presentable, but the pups still didn't have any use for it.

By now the doghouse had become a quirky topic of conversation when friends came over to visit. One close friend of my wife was a professional dog trainer, and she offered this advice:

"The puppies don't want to go in the doghouse because it's like the inside of a cold barn. If you subdivide it into rooms, it would be warmer and cozier."

So I spent the following weekend converting the Godzilla doghouse into a dog apartment building, using plywood to create an internal hallway with a room on each side. As a finishing touch I carpeted the whole inside floor. What was initially a freebie had wound up costing serious money.

The German Shepherds eventually got accustomed to the doghouse and even used it from time to time to get out of a heavy rainstorm.

In 1969 we put our home up for sale. One day Joanne and I were giving some potential buyers a tour of the property. In the backyard the couple stared at the doghouse quizzically.

I told them, "It would make an excellent shelter for your family in the event of a bad earthquake. Or you could rent it out to college students."

৪০৫৪

LOCK YOUR DOORS!

I was signing books at Elaine's Place in Ishpeming. A police officer came in and asked Elaine to be on the lookout for stolen articles from the burglary of a nearby house. He told us that the number of burglaries is on the increase, the main reason being that people in the U.P.—trusting souls that we are—tend to leave doors unlocked.

I lived in Los Angeles for many years, and one thing you never do out there is leave the house unlocked when you go out. The place will likely be picked clean by the time you return. Or worse, a family of homeless persons may have moved in while you were gone.

Naturally, I had to learn this the hard way. The following incidents are absolutely true and illustrate the wisdom of keeping your doors locked.

In 1958 my first wife, Emily, and I had just moved out to California. We rented a small house in Santa Monica, and being fresh from Michigan we didn't give much thought to keeping the door locked. One summer night a heavy rainstorm lulled us into an early sleep.

I woke with a start. Emily was screeching in my ear. "Someone's in the house!"

I bolted upright. The dark silhouette of a man was framed by the bedroom door.

"Get outta here!" I shouted bravely from the safety of the bed.

The man turned and went into the living room.

Totally nude, I scrambled out of bed and began putting on my clothes.

"What are you doing?" Emily shouted. "A robber is stealing our stuff, and you're getting dressed?"

I zipped up my pants and ran into the living room. The "robber" was passed out on the couch, blowing stale beer bubbles from a half-open sour-smelling mouth. The front door—apparently left unlocked—was wide open.

By now gallons of adrenalin were surging through my body. I grabbed the guy by the collar and the seat of his pants, dragged him out the front door and pitched him over the porch railing into a clump of bushes below.

I closed and locked the door and went back to the bedroom. Emily was sitting up in bed, holding the blanket up in front of her. "What happened?"

"It was some old drunk getting in out of the rain. I threw him over the porch railing."

Emily jumped out of bed and began putting her clothes on. "You threw him off the porch? He might be hurt."

We went out on the porch and peered over the railing. Our intruder wasn't there.

"Good," I said. "He's gone."

Emily pointed down the street. "I bet he went down to Santa Monica Blvd. Let's go and see if he's all right."

You have to understand that I was very much in love with this woman, which was why I went along with every cockamamie idea that percolated in her cute little head. We put on raincoats and walked the half block to Santa Monica Blvd.

Sure enough, our man was there on a bus-stop bench, hunched over to keep the rain from running down the back of his dirty shirt. Now more sober, he recognized me immediately and threw his arms up to shield his face from any punches I might throw.

My wife put a hand on his shoulder. "We're not going to hurt you. Do you have any money?"

He looked at her warily, then shook his head. Emily put her hand out to me. "Do you have any cash?"

I reached into my pocket and pulled out two dollars, the total extent of our disposable funds for the rest of the week. She grabbed both dollars and handed them to the guy. "Go to a restaurant and buy a sandwich and cup of coffee so you can get out of the rain."

I shook my head as we walked back home. A guy breaks into my house, and I wind up buying him dinner.

In the late sixties my second wife, Joanne, and I were living in Hermosa Beach, California. One summer we went on a camping trip in Oregon. When we returned home we found the front door ajar.

"Didn't you lock the door when we left?" Joanne asked.

"I thought you locked it," I countered defensively.

We walked in to find all kinds of papers—canceled checks, bank statements, old bills, etc:—scattered over the living-room floor. Someone had been searching for cash. We'd been burglarized.

We rushed from room to room to access what the burglars had taken. Our hi-fi stereo tape recorder and speakers hadn't been touched. My twelve-string guitar was still there.

"Oh no! They've taken all my clothes!" Joanne yelled from the bedroom.

I ran in there and found that all my clothes were also gone. Why the burglars stole used clothing and left hi-fi equipment and a guitar was something I never quite figured out.

For a minute or two we agonized over the loss. Then I got to thinking. "Y'know, this is covered by our insurance."

Joanne's eyes brightened. "You mean . . ."

"Yeah. The insurance company gives us a check, and we can go out and get all new clothes."

I should point out that we didn't buy our clothes on Rodeo Drive in Beverly Hills. We usually waited till Sears was having a big sale before we went clothes shopping. The sports coats that I wore to work were pure synthetic fabrics that would melt under a hot sun. Any settlement from the insurance company would result in a major upgrade to our wardrobe.

I opened a couple of beers to celebrate our good fortune in being burglarized. "The first thing we have to do though, is report the theft to the police." I put down my beer and made the call.

"I think you're in luck," the police dispatcher said. "Yesterday we nabbed a couple of guys driving a stolen car. The trunk of the car was filled with clothes. Come down to the station and see if they're yours."

We went down to the police station. Sure enough, heaped in one large grubby pile was all of our clothes. Nothing was missing. Instead of a brand new wardrobe we were facing a humongous dry-cleaning bill.

Joanne was heartbroken. "They put their loot in the trunk of a STOLEN car," she muttered, pawing through the dirty blouses in the pile. "Just our luck! We had to have our house knocked over by the dumbest burglars on the planet."

⅘⅚

ORANGE-BARREL BLUES

Picture this: A Chicago family on their summer vacation is driving in the U.P.

Wife "Harry, you wanted to come up here so we could enjoy the scenery and breathe in fresh, clean air. But this fresh, clean air smells like TAR."

Husband "Yeah, well, at least it's FRESH tar."

And it surely is. Road repair—our alternate season to winter—is in full swing. All over the U.P. the atmosphere is brimming with the tangy aroma of newly minted asphalt. This time of year you see more orange traffic barrels than pine trees. Lines of cars extending beyond the curvature of the earth wait patiently for a gum-chewing teenager in a hard hat to get off the cell phone and flip over the red STOP sign to SLOW.

During a U.P. summer you can't estimate the time it takes to get from point A to point B. A few weeks ago I was driving to a book signing in Mackinaw City. I had it all figured out. Leave Marquette at 10AM to get to Seney—the halfway point—around noon for a nice leisurely lunch at the Seney Crossroads Restaurant. After several road-repair stops and many miles of reduced speed limits on M-28 I arrived at Seney closer to 1PM only to find that the road ahead to Newberry was going to be even slower.

I had excellent lunch service at the Seney Crossroads Restaurant because there were practically no other customers. They couldn't get to the restaurant. That morning a road crew had freshly paved Highway M-28 in both directions, all the way through the town of Seney, neatly blocking off every roadside business on the highway. The only way to get to the restaurant was to cross fresh asphalt on the eastbound lane. I may have broken the law as I edged the Subaru across, leaving faint tire tracks across the new road surface. But there was no other way. MDOT may now have me on their ten-most-wanted list.

Following the quick lunch I made a detour of my own, south to US-2. I barely made it to Mackinaw City in time for the book signing.

I wonder if anyone has ever put a price tag on the economic impact of all the road repair work up here during the summer. I'll bet it's enormous. Every roadside business suffers when the paving crews block access to their door. Some go belly-up because summer is their make or break season. Many tourists avoid the U.P. completely because they don't want to be dodging all that heavy equipment rumbling around.

There's got to be a better way to maintain roads, and as a matter of fact I've come up with one.

Go back to dirt roads.

Think about it. All they'd have to do is grade the roads once or twice a week to keep them smooth. It doesn't require much heavy equipment and it's quick. Imagine what could be done with the many millions of dollars saved by not laying down expensive layers of asphalt on each road every few years. The money could finance every high school, college and university in the U.P. And there'd probably be enough cash left over to provide daily complimentary pasties and beer to all needy persons. Or a free sauna for every camp.

Dirt roads would slow down traffic, but that's a plus as far as I'm concerned. There'd be a lot less people getting banged up or killed, and you'd save a ton of money on auto insurance. Besides, I think it would be quite tranquil poking along on a dirt road.

Tourists would love it. Dirt roads would make us more quaint than we already are. Visitors like Mackinac Island because there are no cars. They think it's a kick walking cobblestone streets, having to dodge horse droppings.

Okay, dirt roads have mud puddles, but that could work to our advantage. Remember how much fun it was to splash through mud puddles when we were kids? We could turn them into tourist attractions.

DRIVE THROUGH THE LARGEST MUD PUDDLE IN
NORTH AMERICA—2 MILES AHEAD

One alternate suggestion. Last week I pulled onto the shoulder of M-28 and took a closeup look at one of those orange traffic barrels. They're made in California. It must cost the state of Michigan big bucks to have them manufactured and freighted from California. We could easily underbid those yahoos out there, get the orange barrel contract, and give our state's economy a shot in the arm. If we were making them right here we'd feel a lot better about dodging those fool things on the highway.

ഔഈ

PSEUDO WIVES

When I was a young man I had a severe inferiority complex when it came to women. I was awkward and clumsy around girls and never knew what to say on dates. Sometimes I'd make up a list of things to talk about before I picked up the girl, but if the date lasted longer than anticipated, I'd exhaust my list and clam up like a wooden sphinx. Saddled with this affliction, I was convinced that I'd never find a woman who'd consider me a suitable candidate for marriage.

But in my senior year at the U of M I somehow did find such a woman, and we were married in 1957. I thanked the good Lord for starting me off on a lifetime of eternal bliss.

But a few short months later I began wondering: "What in the *(@%%#!! have I gotten myself into?"

When I was single, and wanted to go out for a beer I'd just put on my jacket, head for the door and that was it. Now I had this harsh female inquisitor wanting to know in a shrill voice where I thought I was going to find the money to buy beer.

And she was right. Being married there *WASN'T* any money for beer, which was strange because I'd never had any financial problems when I was single. The old adage that two can live as cheaply as one is a piece of fiction invented by some bridal-shop owner.

Lack of money and a host of other assorted unpleasantries led to the dissolution of that marriage in 1960.

And did I learn my lesson? Of course not. In 1964, during a period of temporary insanity, I married another woman, and that union pretty much went down the same slippery slope as the first debacle. Finally, by 1971 I rejoined the bachelor ranks and swore off marriage forever.

So for all these years I've remained unattached, and that's as it should be. I'm basically selfish and lazy. I enjoy living by myself, don't even have pets. My tenet for a happy life is not being responsible for anything that eats.

My life moves along at a serene pace, no problems, no stress. However, matrimony must have permanently twisted some neural pathway in my brain responsible for good sense because periodically I get this inexplicably mysterious yearning to have some woman around to provide a recall of married life. Nothing permanent, mind you, I just need a quick reminder from time to time.

I've found the solution. Pseudo wives. Pseudo wives are women who impinge on my life for a short time, remind me of what I'm missing by being single, and then make an exit. I'm not talking about sex. Sex is pleasant. Pseudo wives get in my face and tell me things like it's time I changed shirts, got a haircut, or just give me a hard time for no reason at all.

Kerri Rolstone comes over to my place every two weeks, cleans my apartment, does my laundry, and shops for my groceries. Kerri's been doing this for so many years that she pretty much takes charge when she walks in the door. She usually demands enough grocery money to get, for instance, three twelve-packs of Mountain Dew instead of just the one I need because they might be on sale this week. She shows me one of my shirts that she just washed but still has a stain on the front and wants to know what the heck I spilled on it. Kerri gazes around my office which is pretty much a depository for stuff I don't know what else to do with. She shakes her head and says it's time I got rid of that junk because she's tired of straightening it up. If I'm stretching out on the recliner while she's cleaning, Kerri sticks her head in the living-room door and snaps, "Are you napping again?"

So you see, this woman gives me a sobering flashback of day-to-day married life. But what's really great is I simply write out a check for her services and she goes away for two weeks.

I frequently go over to Peggy Sue's Cafe in Ishpeming and have lunch with my friend, Jeff. Dee and Penny are the two regular waitresses, a more crusty sarcastic pair you'll never meet. Sometimes when I take my cap off Dee scowls and tells me to go into the men's room and comb my hair. If Jeff makes a smart remark to Penny, she'll likely cuff him across the back of the head and then tells me to stop grinning or I'll get one too. Dee puts a tall glass of water in front of me and tells me that I'd better drink every drop before I leave. Penny looks down and checks out our socks to make sure they match. One day I was walking out the door when I felt a sharp tug. Dee had pulled a Wal-Mart sales tag off the back of my new khakis, wanting to know if I ever looked in the mirror before I went outside in the morning.

But Jeff and I pay the bill, leave a tip on the table and go home. We won't be badgered by these two until the next time we decide to eat there. (Seriously, I've eaten in restaurants all over the world, and Dee and Penny are the best servers I've ever run across. Incidently, Peggy Sue's has excellent food.)

So these are my pseudo wives. I only see them as often as necessary to quench the curious need to reacquaint myself with married life. Pseudo wives may cost a few bucks, but compared to financing a full-time real wife it's cheap at ten times the price.

😐∞😑

THE ECONOMICS OF DEER HUNTING

E ver since man has walked erect on the face of the earth, he's hunted game to provide food for his family. Through the ages this has been true and remains so, even today. Every November tens of thousands of deer hunters trek into the forests to put venison on the table during the coming winter.

Since so many deer hunters take to the woods every fall, hunting must still be an economical means of providing food. After all, a full-grown deer will put meat on the table for a long time. But modern life is more complex than in times past, so let's take a look at the needs of today's hunter during a typical two-week deer season to reassure ourselves that hunting still makes economic sense. Your intrepid reporter (me, who else?) painstakingly conducted thorough research on this subject.

You must have a deer license, which is really quite a bargain at $15. Now for the equipment. I explored Gander Mountain in Marquette and found a nice Savage 30-06 rifle with scope for only $400. A box of twenty cartridges ran $26, but the new rifle has to properly sighted in, so I'd recommend two boxes of ammunition.

Good visibility is essential during a deer hunt, and Gander Mountain had a proper tree stand for $100. While you're sitting on the tree stand, a simple $5 deer call can make all the difference to a successful hunt. If you bring down your buck far from camp, a wheeled deer cart will come in mighty handy; they run about $80. In the event of unseasonably deep snow, a pair of snowshoes ($125) will be essential. To dress out your kill you'll need a long sharp knife ($75). And aside from the wintery weather, the U.P. woods can truly be a forbidding place if a hunter becomes lost. A Meridian GPS locator at $400 is definitely a worthwhile investment to insure a safe return to camp.

Let's talk about clothes. Because deer hunters spend long periods of time sitting or standing in cold weather, warm attire is a must. Gander Mountain had an insulated waterproof fleece parka and bib for only $250. A warm cap, gloves, and sweater are also needed ($100). A set of high-quality underwear specifically designed for low activity level in cold conditions runs about $80. Footwear is extremely important. Heavy thermal socks and a pair of 600-gram zip boots with Gore-Tex liners will come to $160.

Staying at deer camp has been a time-honored tradition in the U.P., as it should be. Hunters have the need to assemble together to compare hunting strategies. Deer camps are in remote locations, so transportation costs must be considered. A roof rack ($200) for your SUV will be necessary to carry your buck home. $100 will probably cover gasoline expenses. Adequate provisions must be laid in for the entire two-week season. Plenty of hi-energy foods such as pancakes, eggs, beef steaks, fried potatoes, and pasties are important to sustain the hunter throughout the grueling hunt. Allow for a grocery bill of about $500 for each hunter at deer camp for the entire two weeks. A good wine goes well with a hearty dinner. For each hunter ten bottles at $30 apiece should cover it.

After a hard day's hunt, it's essential to relax at camp in the evening. Beer is excellent for relaxing. Every hunter should bring his share of four cases of beer ($50) to camp. Another good idea is soothing bedtime reading material such as *Playboy, Penthouse,* and *Hustler* ($25).

After several days out at deer camp, many hunters crave more social interaction than the fellowship of their hunting companions. Relaxing at a pub in the nearest town might be just the ticket. Hunters will often strike up conversations in the tavern with wives or girl friends of hunters in other deer camps. These women also desire social companionship, and a friendly gesture is buy to them a cocktail or two. Budget about $400 for these junkets into town.

Every venture, regardless of careful planning, has its setbacks, and deer hunting is no exception. It sometimes happens that after an evening of perhaps somewhat excessive relaxation in camp that a hunter's physical coordination is not the best the following morning. Allow $250 for a visit to the nearest hospital emergency room to treat minor injuries sustained due to falling from the tree stand.

Another setback is when a hunter, relaxing in a dimly lit pub, mistakenly buys his own wife a cocktail. In this case it's wise to budget in $3000 for marriage counseling fees.

So, you see, there are some expenses associated with modern-day deer hunting, but, of course, don't forget the reward. If the hunter bags even just an average-size buck, there will be as much as *FIFTY POUNDS* of meat. Think of that, fifty pounds of delicious venison! Just for fun, let's compute the cost per pound to see how economical this meat is. Let's see...take the total deer-hunting cost of $6567, divide by fifty and we get our venison at...

$131.00 a pound.

Hmmm . . . wait a minute . . . can that be right? . . . Let me crunch those numbers again . . .

෧෬

CONFESSIONS OF A COMPUTER DUMMY

During the early sixties I was working for the newly formed Aerospace Corporation in Southern California. My job as section manager in the Computation Department was to interface with engineers in other parts of the company to create computer models of aerospace weapons systems that the U.S. military had interest in at the time. If someone needed to know the ablation profile of a warhead reentering the atmosphere, they would come to my office and hand me a set of equations. I'd then sit down with one of the programmers in my section and discuss the creation of a computer model to do the job. The programmer would go off and begin coding up the model.

This all sounds hugely scientific, precise, and very straightforward, right? In fact, that wasn't quite the way it worked. What I really spent most of my time doing was helping programmers figure out why their scientific, precise, carefully programmed computer models crashed and burned each time they tried to execute them. Every morning wrought-up people in my section literally formed a line outside my office door, clutching computer printouts, wanting to know what went wrong. I would scan the hard-copy printouts—dumps of the computer's memory when the trouble occurred—and tell them what the problem was.

I was very good at this troubleshooting, mainly because I did it day in and day out. I could read a computer octal memory dump like a Mickey Spillane novel. At the risk of sounding immodest, I was a computer expert of that era. Of course, keep in mind that digital computers back then had vacuum tubes, needed dedicated air-conditioning systems to function properly, had small memories, and were fairly slow. Today your grandson's PC would calculate rings around them.

For thirty-some years I was involved with aerospace-applications computers of one type or another. These machines all had unique architectures, operating systems, and languages. Every time I got involved with a new computer I had to take home a stack of manuals to get smart on it.

When I retired in 1993 I took great pleasure thinking that I no longer had to read technical manuals on military communication-satellite software or pore over operating-system manuals for on-board computers of the Titan IV launch vehicles. I'd had enough. I was going to devote full time to my second career—humor writing—and get entirely out of the computer business.

Well, that didn't happen entirely. At the time I retired, PC's were becoming immensely popular with the American public, and being a writer I had to have one. But did I buy a PC, take it home and learn how to set it up myself? Absolutely not. That would have involved reading instruction manuals. I hired a computer guru, had him open up the cartons, plug the cables together, and get the thing running. I learned only the minimum I needed to know, which was basic word processing so I could write stories.

For twelve years I've diligently ignored the technical progress in computers. In 1999 I had to get a new PC in order to access the Internet to do research for my stories and columns. But again I hired a local guru to bring the new machine to my apartment, hook it up, and show me how to use the Internet.

This PC came with a curious little gadget called a mouse. When I pushed the mouse around the desk top a little white arrow scooted across the PC monitor screen. This was supposed to be handy to use with the new software called WINDOWS. I pointed the arrow at a little picture called a icon on the WINDOWS screen, and all kinds of weird stuff appeared. For example, one box flashed up, telling me that my Ethernet Adapter was a Novell 2000 with an adapter address of 00-00-B4-3B-71, an IP address of 24.177.155.177, a subnet mask of 255.255.240.0 and a default gateway of 24.177.144.1. What I'd like to know is what is this stuff, do I need to know it, and what did I pay for it?

Twelve years of not reading computer manuals, and I don't know what anything is anymore. I see words like digerati, servlet, sysop, podcasting, perl . . . I have no idea what they mean. Is MOO a verb or a noun? Is an applet a small apple? Probably not. The problem is that today's computer technology has been taken over by teenagers who speak in tongues.

These days everybody's becoming a blogger. I might even be a blogger myself, but I don't have a firm idea what a blogger is. The whole thing has become really embarrassing. Forty years ago I was a computer expert, and now I'm a computer dummy. I used to tell programmers how to solve complex computer problems, and now I know less about computers than your average fourth grader.

To make matters worse I might need another new PC. My six-year-old PC—a doddering geezer by computer standards–has begun acting up. Every so often it just freezes. The only thing that makes it go is when I kill the power and start it up again. A person much younger than myself told me that I should "defrag" the PC. I'd be happy to do that if I knew what "defragging" is. Could somebody please send one of their grandchildren over to my place? I need help.

ॐ

RADIO DAYS

T he other day, over lunch at Peggy Sue's Café, my friend, Jeff, and I somehow got on the topic of old-time radio programs. We quickly became embroiled in a struggle to see who knew the most trivia on 1940's radio programs. Jeff finally brought me to my knees by rattling off the names of the Allen's Alley residents on the Fred Allen program. (How many of you remember Senator Claghorn, Mrs. Nussbaum, and Titus Moody?)

Come to think of it, if you're under the age of fifty there's no point reading any further; you're too young to know what I'm talking about.

When I was a kid, radio was our TV, the prime source of entertainment for the whole family. Most evenings my parents, sister, Esther, and I gathered around the radio. We all listened to the same programs because in those days everything was G-rated.

Interestingly, radios back then were quite powerful and consequently pricey. And my father bought the very best. We had a huge floor-model Zenith that, in 1940, cost over fifty dollars. In today's dollars that would be around fifteen hundred. The host of vacuum tubes inside that radio threw enough heat to warm up our whole living room in the winter. But it could pick up stations from the four corners of the earth, including ships and airplanes. One night the old man got Radio Havana, and we all sat there and listened to an hour of news in Spanish, although none of us understood a word of it.

First on my radio-listening schedule were the kid serials in the late afternoon. Each program lasted only fifteen minutes, so between four and six o'clock there were a lot of them. Leading off was "Jack Armstrong, the All American Boy" who, with high-school chums, Billy and Betty, thwarted evildoers all over the globe.

Captain Midnight and his Secret Squadron flew their piston-engine airplanes here and there, constantly trying to foil plans of the ruthless Ivan Shark. The sponsor, Ovaltine, informed young listeners that mailing in the foil top from their product would guarantee membership in the Secret Squadron. Having an airplane wasn't a requirement.

I also remember following the adventures of "Hop Harrigan," "The Shadow," "Sky King," and "Terry and the Pirates." *The Flight of the Bumblebee* introduced "The Green Hornet" and his trusty companion, Kato. This was followed by the final serial of the afternoon–my favorite–"The Lone Ranger," galloping into the living room on his great horse, Silver. About this time my mother was calling me into the kitchen for supper. I'd bolt my food down and rush back to the radio so as not to miss the Lone Ranger's latest adventure. If you're having dinner with me sometime and notice that I've finished way ahead of you, the Lone Ranger is at the bottom of it.

Who could forget "Fibber McGee and Molly," brought to you by Johnson's Wax? Fibber was the original BS artist who would get into verbal jousting matches with his neighbor and archrival in baloney shoveling, Throckmorton P. Gildersleeve. But the highlight of the program was Fibber inadvertently opening the door to the hall closet and promptly getting buried beneath an avalanche of "stuff." These were live broadcasts, and I always wondered how they created the sound of two tons of household goods cascading out of the closet.

During the war Walter Winchell gave us the war news in a staccato delivery of about 200 words a minute . How many of you remember his opening: "Good evening Mister and Mrs. North America and all the ships at sea."

My mother took over the dial when the "Royal Gelatin Hour," starring Rudy Vallee, came on. Before Bing Crosby, Rudy Vallee was the original "crooner." I never cared much for Rudy, but my mother gushed over him every week.

Saturday-night fare included "Your Hit Parade," brought to you by Lucky Strike cigarettes. This was back in the days when cigarette companies could advertise in the media. "Your Hit Parade" played the most popular songs of that week, based on sheet-music sales and juke-box play. They secretly held the top three songs for the end of the program, and the four of us made out paper ballots with our guesses at those top three to see who was the most music-savvy one in the family.

The one radio program that I frequently didn't hear the end of was "Inner Sanctum Mysteries." Inner Sanctum began with the sound of a doorknob turning slowly, then the horrific creaking of an obviously large door, followed by a sinister "Good evening," uttered by their host, Raymond. Raymond told stories of insane murderers, ghosts, and other eerie creatures of the night. If Raymond was really on his game I'd get so scared that I'd voluntarily go to bed early. The old man loved Inner Sanctum, but my mother didn't have much use for it. Every week she'd say, "Why don't they oil the hinges on that door?"

Charlie McCarthy and his ventriloquist sidekick, Edgar Bergen, had the prime slot on Sunday evenings, sponsored by Chase & Sanborn coffee–"good to the last drop." In 1940 Charlie McCarthy was as famous as Paris Hilton is now, but maybe a little brainier. I also loved Mortimer Snerd who played second dummy on the program.

But my absolute favorite was "The Jack Benny Show,"

sponsored by J-E-L-L-O. Jack Benny was an absolute master at comic timing, and on the program he portrayed a fictional miserly version of himself. Jack's severely underpaid valet, Rochester, would chauffeur him around in a ramshackle, antique Maxwell automobile that precipitously wheezed and rattled down the street whenever they took it out. Every so often Jack would decide to visit his money which was at the end of a tunnel in a vault buried deep beneath the streets of Beverly Hills. The vault was guarded by an old-timer who never saw the light of day and depended on Jack to tell him what was going on in the world.

With the exception of Public Radio's "Car Talk" on Saturday mornings, I don't listen to radio much anymore. There's nothing on. One day while driving to Ishpeming I surfed the AM dial to see what I could find. Nothing but hard-rock stations. Do any of you understand the words in those songs? Would I *WANT* to understand the words? Are there actually words?

℘〇℘

Biography

Jerry Harju was born in Ishpeming, Michigan, in 1933. He received a degree in engineering from the University of Michigan in 1957 and an MS from the University of Southern California in 1985. After thirty years as a manager in the Southern California aerospace industry, Jerry began writing as a second career. *Northern Reflections, Northern D'Lights, Northern Passages,* and *Northern Memories* are collections of humorous short stories about growing up in the Upper Peninsula in the 1930's and 40's.

The Class of '57 humorously describes Jerry's six years of "higher education" at the University of Michigan. University life then—with its 1950's attitudes on world affairs, morality, and women's roles in society—was much different from today. *Cold Cash* is Jerry's first novel, a wacky tale about two amateurs who try to solve their cash-flow problems by pulling a bank heist and getting away on snowmobiles. Typical of Harju's work, the robbery doesn't go as planned and is further complicated by two strong-willed women. The book won a Midwest Independent Publishers Association Book Achievement Award. *Here's what I think... , Way Back When,* and his latest, *Our World was in Black and White* are collections of selected humorous and nostalgic essays appearing for the past several years in the Marquette newspaper, the *Mining Journal.*

In addition to writing books, newspaper and magazine columns, and running a publishing company, Jerry travels all over the globe.